The Mighty Advisor

How thought disruptors
galvanise leaders and
reshape organisations

TONY SEDGWICK

R^ethink

First published in Great Britain in 2021
by Rethink Press (www.rethinkpress.com)

Picture credits
p42: Wellcome Collection / CC BY-NC 4.0
p88: Inigo Lopez Vazquez / CC BY-SA 4.0
p133: Fimon006 / CC BY-SA 3.0
p153: emilegraphics / the Noun Project

Mighty Advisor Illustrations by Jeremy Duncan.

All other images are public domain.

Contents

'This man penetrates my secret thoughts; he knows things that I have only communicated to a few people.'

— Duke Frédéric Maurice de la Tour D'Auvergne (1605–1652)

Prologue: The Encounter

I was summoned to a meeting in room twenty-five at headquarters at eleven o'clock. That was all I knew – the memo (in those pre-email days) said nothing about who I was supposed to meet or why. What's more, it wasn't a question of simply getting into a taxi or on a train – HQ was in another country. But I'd received direction from my head of department, so I had to go.

I got a flight and arrived at the door of room twenty-five at the appointed hour. I knocked and the door was opened by a towering figure wearing baggy trousers held up with red braces. He introduced himself as Otis; I would have put him at about sixty years old. He had a unique aura that, for some reason, put me instantly at ease: the energy he radiated seemed to open an invisible neural connection between our two minds. I felt we were in a bubble of trust, and I found I could not stop talking; I so wanted to engage with him and tell him all about myself and my work.

To this day, I don't understand what happened during that meeting; all I know is that it was a delightful experience. The time flew by and when this extraordinary encounter was over, I was desperate to talk to someone about it. The person I spoke to seemed underwhelmed by my account: 'Oh yes, that's Otis,' he said, nonchalantly. 'He used to be George Bush's advisor. He walks around the building meeting people. He's been hired as some sort of *éminence grise*.' This hardly seemed to account for the experience I'd just had, but I'd never heard the term before, so I headed to the library to look it up. *Éminence grise* was defined as: 'A person who exercises power or influence in a certain sphere without holding an official position.' To me, it was magical term that encapsulated the wonder of my encounter. I had a feeling that if I could find out more about the *éminence grise*, I would have my finger on the pulse of my organisation.

L'Éminence Grise by Jean-Léon Gérôme (1873)

Introduction

From my first encounter with an *éminence grise*, I was determined to find out what it meant to occupy that position. How is it that they can wield so much influence? What qualities do these people have? These questions occupied my thoughts for many years.

The original *éminence grise*, I discovered, was one Father Joseph du Tremblay, advisor to Cardinal Richelieu, Chief Minister to Louis XIII of France from 1624 to 1642. Where Richelieu was resplendent in his scarlet robes and was known, because of this and his cardinal's title, as the *Éminence Rouge*, du Tremblay wore the humble grey habit of a Capuchin monk and was therefore dubbed *Éminence Grise*.

It is Aldous Huxley, with his profound interest in philosophy and mythology, who has written the most comprehensive account of this literally shadowy figure. In *Grey Eminence* (1941),[1] he describes Father Joseph as an intuitive man with a blend of extraordinary skills who could connect with others in a way that seemed almost magical.

I have been on the trail of similarly powerful yet elusive figures for decades now, examining their modus operandi, their ways of thinking and behaving, and studying their skills with a view to offering insight and provocation to leaders

---

1   A Huxley, *Grey Eminence*

and organisations in the same way. It's been a uniquely rewarding journey and one I know will never cease.

Most recently, former prime minister Sir John Major used a phrase that crystallised for me the role I had been trying to define. In commenting on perhaps the most sensational UK news story of 2020, that of special advisor Dominic Cummings's infamous trip to Durham, Major suggested that Boris Johnson should get rid of his 'overmighty advisors'.[2] It occurred to me that the term 'Mighty Advisor', however, described very well the power and status of these unelected individuals and could be extended to refer to all those who sit at the side of leaders, both in government and the corporate world.

These people tend to turn up when you least expect them; the trick is to recognise them when you meet them and to acknowledge their significance. They have the power to revolutionise your plans and send you off in a different direction, but through illumination rather than coercion.

My story

My quest to understand the force field of these figures and how they interact with both organisations and individuals has taken me a long way from the career that I originally had in mind.

---

2   A Walker, 'John Major takes aim at Dominic Cummings for "poisoning" politics'

As a child, I was surrounded by storytellers and a couple of inspirational aunties who stimulated my interest in the magic of life. I was always after the big picture, and in trying to capture it I was always asking the tiresome question, 'Why?' This didn't always go down well with my teachers. I was also fascinated by the lotions and potions my mother gave me, such as aspirin, or cream rubbed onto a graze. What was in them? How did they work?

This was what originally set me off on the path to becoming a scientist. I was lucky enough to do my training in experimental pathology at St Bartholomew's Hospital, where I met Professor Derek Willoughby, an expert in the field of inflammation. It was the stories he told me in his office, as he chain-smoked his way through a packet of Embassy, that inspired me more than anything that took place in the lab. A disruptive spirit bursting with new ideas, he taught me to be a lover of life as well as an academic scientist. He took an approach that I've come to call 'working backwards'. Rather than gathering data and making a story from it, he would posit a grand theory and ask provocative questions about it.

Once my training was complete, I moved on and, after a spell teaching at the Royal Veterinary College, I began working in the pharmaceutical industry for a large multi-national in their discovery, business and development organisation. As worldwide head of clinical operations, I was part of a group that discovered groundbreaking treatments for several diseases. But there was no getting away from the fact that my work was becoming more to do with people than with science, and this didn't change when I went on to lead four biotechnology companies.

More recently I've been working with a range of biotech and pharma companies, advising on overall R&D and helping their CEOs and CSOs to pursue their leadership agendas. Through deploying a wide range of skills and providing holistic advice, I can penetrate the grey matter of the leader, anticipating and giving shape to their ambitions. I've realised that strategy starts and ends in the heads of the senior leaders and that, though many people call themselves strategy advisors, they do not have direct access to the mind of the leader.

My approach embraces both a macro and a micro view of human beings. In my work on systemic constellations (see Chapter 7 for information about this discipline), I seek to understand people's place in their family, in their community and in the wider world. But as a scientist, I'm familiar with a magnified view of the most minute elements of the body down the barrel of a microscope. As a teacher of martial arts and of yoga, my focus is on achieving physical, mental and spiritual balance.

A polymath

As you can see, I've found it impossible to confine myself to a straightforward scientific career path. There are just too many connections to be made along the way and the individuals I've found the most impressive have always demonstrated an eclectic mixture of interests and knowledge. For example, the head of R&D at Roche was someone who knew as much about ballet as he did about science. To misquote Shakespeare, there are more things in heaven and earth... than are dreamt of in your MBA syllabus!

An idea that I kept returning to time and again was that of the Renaissance man – the polymath who is interested, and probably proficient, in many different things. If you're boxed in, you can't integrate. You can't see the whole, the *Gestalt*, to use a term borrowed from psychology. I felt there was no point in my understanding the composition of a drug type if I hadn't grasped exactly how it interacted with the whole body and mind.

What I'm interested in is the cross-fertilisation of multiple skills. I like to think of myself as having a rucksack that I travel around with and can delve into to find the appropriate idea or proposal when it's needed. Building a rucksack is essential – the true polymath has a large rucksack with varied contents!

It's important to see the potential connections in the apparently unconnected – something David Bowie was alluding to when he said of himself, 'What I'm best at doing is synthesising those things in society or culture, refracting those things...'[3] In other words, you take multiple angles and you try to triangulate them.

---

3   F Whately (director), *David Bowie*

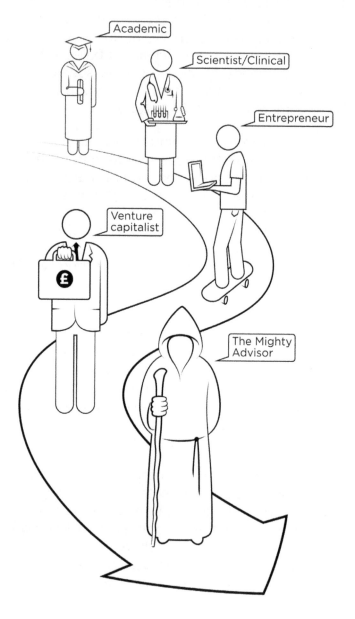

My own journey towards becoming a Mighty Advisor

Behind the veil

I've always imagined that there is a lot more to life than meets the eye. Behind most structures there is a hidden architecture, or a flow of activity that goes unnoticed. This has nothing to do with conspiracy theories; it's a spontaneous phenomenon rather than anything deliberate.

I've seen a whole range of companies up close; some of them were a mess, but others displayed excellence in the way they operated. I often imagined that there was a magic door in such companies that I could simply open and behind it find all the clever people driving its success. It was when I met Otis that the penny dropped: these people really exist. The more time I spent observing organisations or reading literature or mythology, the more I saw these individuals cropping up.

The organisations that are struggling are not adequately resourced. They don't have anyone outside the hierarchy capable of taking a clear-sighted view of the situation and speaking the truth to those in authority when that truth is something they'd prefer not to hear. The might of the Mighty Advisor stems from them being in a position to do just that. Their position also needs to afford them a panoramic view of the organisation or the situation. From the top of the tree, they can see the lie of the land and understand exactly how the game is being played.

It can indeed be lonely at the top – not in the sense that C-suite individuals lack company, but because they are detached from the operation of their organisation. They can't see everything and what they can see is likely from a specific angle. Yet it wouldn't do for them to say, 'I don't know what I'm doing.' I've witnessed this problem as both a leader within organisations and as a trusted advisor, stimulating leaders with productive thought experiments and nurturing good strategic thinking.

Of course, there are endless resources in a modern organisation – HR, facilities, etc – and the leader can go to any one of them for support, but this support will tend to be limited in scope. What I saw going on in most organisations was a lot of transactional, MBA-type thinking, even though people were working in complex webs of connectivity, driven in part by their automatic reactions to one another. Simple, prescriptive ideas are useful, but they do not get to the heart of matters.

The recognition that I needed to explore the secret hinterland of the workplace is what brought me to organisational psychology and a deep dive into what makes people tick.

Peeling back the layers

When I started working on large integration and change management projects, I would go in to do some due diligence on a business and find I was unpeeling the layers of an onion. Over time, I have been able to hone the questions I ask to get to the true picture quickly. This gives me a working hypothesis to test through my subsequent investigations. This is how you unpack what's really going on in a given setting, to understand who is influencing whom, who is failing to influence whom, and where ideas are coming from. I've also developed a degree of pattern recognition; I've seen particular situations before and I know what they can lead to. It's the Mighty Advisor's responsibility to flag up the consequences of a predictable course of events.

The Mighty Advisor is such a key figure for organisations that I wanted to distil the results of my study of these individuals – and of my experience in this role – into a book that would help leaders and organisations understand their true value and how to get the best out of them. We'll start off by identifying the archetypal qualities that Mighty Advisors share, no matter when they lived, their sphere of activity, or their location in the world. Myth and literature are full of vivid illustrations of the ways in which these figures weave their magic.

We'll then examine some real-life examples across the ages and scrutinise their function in the modern organisation, where hierarchies and siloed disciplines often obscure the big picture. What are the weapons in their armoury? We'll look at some of the tools and techniques they use – sometimes spontaneously, sometimes deliberately – to build trust, yet also to disrupt lazy and conventional patterns of thinking. Finally, we'll explore systems and connectivity, recognising that behind all the overt structures there is a hidden architecture that often eludes even the most attentive of leaders. The Mighty Advisor who can map this connectivity offers real potential for galvanising an organisation.

Missing in action: women

By halfway through this book you may be wondering: where are the women?

I have been able to include a few examples, both from history and from literature but, as in so many spheres, they are greatly outnumbered by men. I think the reasons for this are twofold. First, women's contribution in many fields has been overlooked for centuries and only now is research revealing the paintings, the symphonies, the scientific discoveries that they have been responsible for. In some cases, their authorship has been deliberately concealed. For example, all the works of seventeenth century painter Judith Leyster were once attributed to Frans Hals, so that they could be sold for a higher price.

And what of the woman as muse? The term 'muse' often conjures up an image of a woman whose compelling beauty inspires men's creativity, yet let's not forget that personifications of wisdom were often female: the nine Muses themselves; Pallas Athene, goddess of wisdom, and so on. Wisdom, and especially the kind of wisdom that acknowledges connections between areas of knowledge and expertise, is a key string in the Mighty Advisor's bow.

Prehistory tends to suggest that the dominance of men in the public sphere is relatively recent, but we have no evidence of this. The written word only goes back so far and for many years it, too, was the preserve of men. It's been all too easy, then, to ignore or underplay the diffuse power of those who have, until relatively recently, lacked a public platform.

This is a great loss, and I am at pains to emphasise the importance of feminine energy in my work with leaders. I was brought up chiefly by my mother and two maiden aunts. These women were a formative influence in my life, and I would characterise them as polymath creative types who introduced me to many of the softer skills that complement my harder technocratic skills.

A vantage point

In my role as Mighty Advisor to the organisations I work with, I often picture myself as sitting outside a castle but having significant influence within it. There are wooden outhouses around the castle, where most people live. I am well placed to observe those at the heart of power, the wider community surrounding this hub and the comings and goings between these two groups – and between them and the world beyond.

The value the Mighty Advisor offers to the queen or king of the castle is the insight that this advantageous positioning brings when it is allied to wisdom, experience and the ability to identify the patterns in hidden dynamics. My conversations with those I advise tend to lead to a flash of recognition – a 'click' – as they realise that I 'get' them and their problem. They let their guard down and often acknowledge a lack that they have sensed for some time. Having gained their trust, I'm given 'access all areas': I can talk to anyone. And they will talk back to me. I'm outside the hierarchy, probably a bit eccentric in terms of corporate culture and I'm embedded in the community of the organisation that they want to feel part of. The channels are open for this *éminence grise* to strengthen the hidden architecture of the organisation.

Now it's time to dig deeper into how Mighty Advisors practise their mysterious alchemy...

*The castle metaphor – where in the castle does
the leader and their team sit? The Mighty Advisor has
a different vantage point.*

1

The Mighty Advisor has always existed in our collective consciousness: a distinctive presence in all mythologies, contemporary fictions, and in the modern workplace.

CHAPTER 1

The Archetype Of The Mighty Advisor

The more I looked into the phenomenon of the Mighty Advisor, the more I realised what a specialised role they occupy in an organisation. Their presence in the system goes way beyond anything you could call a job. They bring a specific type of energy to their organisation, but there is more to it than that. I began to think of the Mighty Advisor as a 'phenotype', to borrow a term from biology. It was time to put them under the microscope.

A phenotype is an entity with its own range of unique characteristics, including its shape, development, the way it behaves and the consequences of that behaviour. I realised that whenever I saw a play or read up on mythology, a person with a compelling set of characteristics would appear. The equivalent term in a literary context is 'archetype'. These figures turned up so frequently in narratives that I could not help but be intrigued, especially as they all seemed to have what I describe as a 'metamission': a generic function in the narrative, regardless of the differences in time, place, style and culture. These figures are not discussed in your average MBA book, but pick up Homer or Hans Christian Andersen and you can find them quite quickly.

My musings on archetypes led me to Carl Jung. Jung was both a psychologist and a mystic, and it was he who first used the term 'archetype' to denote universal, deep-rooted and symbolic characters that are, in a way, imprinted on our DNA. Jung proposed that people, as well as having independent minds, have a collective consciousness that recognises common patterns. This collective consciousness allows us as individuals to grow into the societies we are born into. The stories that societies tell themselves reflect these patterns and, whether the stories are old or new, feature a cast of recurring characters.[4]

Jung was considerably influenced by the work of nineteenth century anthropologist and ethnographer Adolf Bastian, who pioneered the concept of the 'psychic unity of mankind', a theory inspired by his study of societies in Africa and south-east Asia.[5] There is further endorsement of these theories in the work of Joseph Campbell, who formulated the concept of 'the hero's journey', arguably the blueprint for all fiction, no matter which culture it stems from.[6] Certain archetypal characters recur in these stories, whether they are, for example, contemporary television series or Ancient Greek myths. The Mighty Advisor is one such character. In folk tales and fairy stories, this figure is often a mysterious mentor who can give the hero talismans or privileged information that will help them in their quest.

4   C Jung, *The Archetypes and the Collective Unconscious*
5   M Fischer, P Bolz and S Kamel, *Adolf Bastian and his Universal Archive of Humanity*
6   J Campbell, *The Hero with a Thousand Faces*

I noticed this figure turning up in businesses, or in the stories that people told about businesses. Physical talismans may no longer be given, and the privileged information may come in the form of unique insights rather than magic words or spells, but the result is the same: these gifts have the potential to change the hero/leader's path. The gifts are also evidence that the Mighty Advisor has the lie of the land mapped clearly in their head.

Everybody must negotiate their way through the snakes and ladders of life and we all, whether we're aware of it or not, look for guidance on to the best route to take. The Mighty Advisor has the potential to reset our direction simply by moving us one degree off centre; the amplification of that one degree into hundreds of degrees brings about a dramatic change of trajectory. In organisational terms, the appearance of the Mighty Advisor in the leader's journey gives them the impetus and the ability to move into another orbit.

Archetypal qualities

As I read up on these figures and came across them in specific organisations, I became more and more curious about the qualities that they shared (and whether these qualities were reflected to any degree in the three people I had hired when I first took up a senior post). I began to make an inventory of their qualities as described in myth and literature, compiling my Mighty Advisor's toolkit.

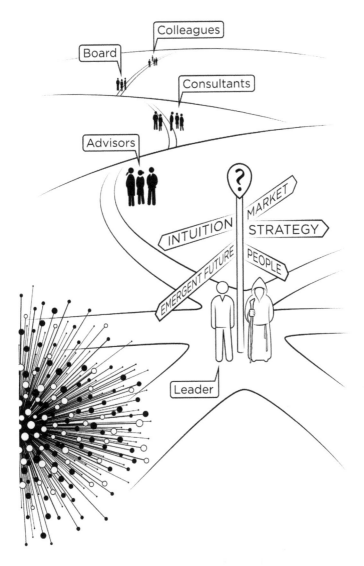

*The leader's journey – when will the Mighty Advisor
turn up to change their trajectory?*

The most prominent characteristic of these figures is that they are truly individuals – archetypes, certainly, but not stock characters like the young naïve hero or the wicked stepmother. This notion of individuals brought me back to the thinking of Carl Jung, for whom individuation – becoming yourself – was a key concept. Individuation entails becoming the most integrated, whole version of yourself: finding the central core that is not affected by social roles and responsibilities. It is this that people respond to. Leaders don't say to themselves specifically, 'I need a Mighty Advisor to help me steer the ship.' 'Mighty Advisor' isn't normally a recognised function within an organisation. They are looking for that particular individual, perhaps even without any awareness of the polymathic skills they bring with them and whether they are relevant to the organisation.

THREE HIRES

When I got my first properly senior post, in charge of several thousand staff, I looked at the range of my responsibilities and decided there were three people I needed to hire.

The first was a psychotherapist. I was exhausted by talking to so many people and wanting to be liked by them. My customary greeting of 'How are you?' to those I passed in the corridor elicited a conversation every time, and after ten of these I was worn out. The psychotherapist helped me to understand people without having to drain my resources.

Second, I engaged a big picture strategist, not to create my strategy for me, but to help me become a strategic thinker.

The third hire was an actor and musician, who taught me about image and public speaking, about how to make an impact.

These three people mitigated the pressure of constant visibility and the need to exhibit clarity and certainty at every moment.

I must emphasise that what a Mighty Advisor doesn't have is a personal brand, something recommended by much MBA thinking. If you picture a set of Russian dolls, personal branding is the one on the outside – you will not find individuation until you're three dolls in. Personal branding is a calculated veneer.

All too often, people have a concept of what constitutes being themselves, onto which they project various assumptions. For the leader, those assumptions might be, 'As a leader, I must have strength and a good critical mind.' The danger is that you get stuck in these life scripts, but the Mighty Advisor is capable of introducing that infinitesimal tilt on one's axis that leads to a radical change of direction. My encounter with Otis was one of those moments: it changed my trajectory.

Charisma

Any consideration of the characteristics shared by Mighty Advisors leads me back to Otis and the qualities he displayed. Above all, he made me feel good. This is the abiding principle that I bring to my own practice: if nothing else, I try to make the people I work with feel better than they did before they knew me. Otis was simply *nice*, and he felt real. Somehow, this added up to charisma. It's an enigmatic quality that is sensed rather than seen. Those with charisma sparkle in a way that has nothing to do with money or power. Their presence in, and psychological dominance of, a room is palpable; they stand out from a two-dimensional picture as fully three-dimensional.

Another quality I have observed in these figures is that they are comfortable in their own skins. Despite their outsider status, they are at ease in whatever setting they find themselves in. They radiate a quiet self-confidence and can transfer that feeling to leaders. The authenticity at their core means they do not seek authentication from anyone else.

When someone who is charismatic and in a position of authority can relate in a genuine way to their subordinates, we refer to them as having the 'common touch'. The Mighty Advisor has both the common touch and the self-assurance needed to interact with leaders.

Diverse talents

These individuals also often possess a surprisingly wide range of abilities and expertise; you could call them multi-disciplinary. They have acquired these capabilities through their experience; through their habit of observing, reflecting and learning; and not least through an innate curiosity that drives them to follow a subject or a line of thought down and across its numerous ramifications.

Bastian himself is a good example of this. He started out as a physician, but then his interest in people, alongside his travels, meant his expertise expanded into ethnology, anthropology, psychology and philosophy.

They may not claim to be experts in every field, but Mighty Advisors know enough to be able to hold their own among experts, challenging them in the context of the bigger picture.

Chameleon-like

As three-dimensional beings, Mighty Advisors are multifaceted. This entails far more than what is now called 'code switching': turning on the right register for the company you are in. Their experience, knowledge, wisdom and wide frame of reference, as described above, make them an empathic resource for anyone who can benefit from their gifts. They can manifest exactly what is needed, when it is needed.

Shamanic traits

The figure of the shaman, the wise person – for they can be male or female – has been present in societies all over the world for thousands of years, and they are imprinted on the DNA of our cultures. They were not the leaders of a clan or tribe, but the pre-eminent source of wisdom and guidance for the leaders. They had practical skills such as healing and problem solving, but also esoteric skills: they were able to cast their minds into other realms, becoming literal visionaries.

Shamans often acquired their knowledge through a vision quest. Their journey was more than a progression from A to B: along the way they would learn new things, meet diverse kinds of people and observe strange phenomena, then bring this wider picture back to their own society. Some of the prehistoric images of creatures that look like animals and humans fused together suggest that there were beings in the midst of human groups who were different – highly individuated and able to maintain the cohesion and direction of the group through their supernatural powers.

Four paradigms

There are further archetypes within the archetype, as Mighty Advisors adopt specific roles. Sometimes they occupy one role permanently, sometimes they adapt to the role that is best suited to their purposes. Even a casual reading of Greek mythology, fairy tales and literature will reveal several basic manifestations of the Mighty Advisor. I've chosen to focus on four of these figures, but there is no set number and many additional archetypes have been proposed by various thinkers since Jung's time. I'll outline some of their main features, then we'll take a closer look at some specific examples of these archetypes.

The trickster

The trickster embodies a strong desire for change and brings it about through creative energy. Their disruptive force breaks open echo chambers and rides roughshod over groupthink. Leaders often find their new and provoking ideas frightening, but such ideas are guaranteed to challenge the status quo.

Tricksters, or jesters, can be cunning or apparently foolish, or both by turns. They're not afraid to openly question or mock authority and they're fond of breaking rules, boasting and playing tricks – does that call anyone to mind?

This archetype is a threat to the system as it generates change, but where the weight of stability encounters the impetus of instability, creative tension arises. The message for organisations is that a complex strategy is sometimes not amenable to reasoning; it needs ideas that may not be forthcoming using traditional step-by-step logic.

*Engraving of a jester
by E Mohn after A Lambron (1875)*

The wise man

This archetype possesses immense knowledge and experience, allied to profound insight. In literature, the wise man often takes the form of a teacher or a mentor. The word 'mentor' in fact comes from the name of the man (literally, Mentor) responsible for educating and guiding Odysseus's son, Telemachus, while Odysseus was away fighting in the Trojan War and taking his time about getting home.

The wise man has great foresight and offers measured advice to the hero to help him on his quest, while often apparently letting him choose his own destiny. Making people believe they've arrived at decisions and discoveries by themselves is one of the subtlest skills of the Mighty Advisor. If you need someone to calm a situation, apply wisdom and experience to the problem at hand and bring hotheads together for rational deliberation, the wise man is the go-to figure. They may also be the repository of organisational memory.

The wanderer

Traditionally, the wanderer is the explorer who sets off on a great journey, without a map, and has adventures in strange lands. Today, such wanderers are often seen as cultural dropouts, living on the margins of society, defining themselves in opposition to the cultural norm. Some could almost be seen as prophets, purveying uncomfortable truths that we acknowledge deep down. Many climate change evangelists belong in this category.

Within organisations, though, the wanderer archetype can be a useful ally. Able to roam freely, the wanderer can view and map the terrain from multiple angles; their exploration is enriched by their conversations with people from every corner and level of the organisation. They are creating the equivalent of an explorer's map, showing not only the topography, but also the hidden dragons. People in organisations may unwittingly open up to them, perceiving that these outsiders have no personal stake in the organisation.

The shapeshifter

The notion of the shapeshifter has its roots in magic, in the notion that there are beings whose precise form and identity cannot be pinned down. They are ambiguous, neither one thing nor the other, unstable and unpredictable. Their protean (after Proteus, a Greek god who symbolised the ever-changing nature of the sea) skills mean that they are never in danger of being confined to organisational silos. They have expertise, but across a range of domains.

In organisational terms, it is all too easy to get ten experts around the table, but then who can integrate their input? The leader may be overburdened with other issues; the shapeshifter can draw together the disparate strands and offer up a coherent picture to the organisation. Often when I go into an organisation, I can see that its design is impeded by the titles of the individuals within it. I may even come across someone who is bringing absolutely the right energy, but the leadership can't quite work out what to do with them because they're hard to pigeonhole.

The Mighty Advisor in fiction

Mythology, folklore and literature offer a rich selection of examples that illustrate a Mighty Advisor in action. Everyone is likely to be familiar with at least one of the figures I describe here, since they feature in both the printed word and on screen.

Svengali

As his name has become a shorthand for a shadowy figure wielding immense power behind the scenes, no examination of the role of Mighty Advisor is complete without mention of Svengali. He appears in the 1895 novel *Trilby* by George du Maurier as a mysterious figure of such compelling hypnotic power that he can turn a tone-deaf Irish laundress into a diva.[7] He may be literally mesmerising, but in the novel Svengali has neither charisma nor integrity and, unfortunately, the book's overt antisemitism and theme of what would doubtless now be understood as coercive control mean that it has not aged well.

---

7   G Du Maurier, *Trilby*

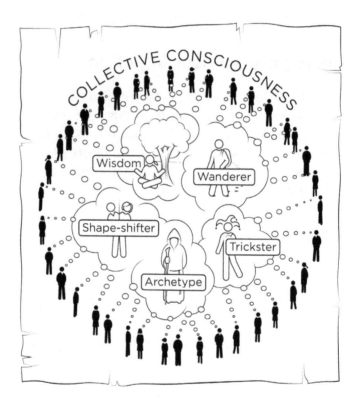

*Archetypes within archetypes – the many
facets of a Mighty Advisor*

Doctor Who

As an enduring figure in popular culture, Doctor Who vividly embodies the shapeshifter and wanderer aspects of the Mighty Advisor. Shapeshifting into an entirely different character is an essential feature of the Doctor – to the point where the role has become female (despite the objections of the more sexist Whovians) – and no one could wander more widely than this traveller in time and space. When you've encountered as many diverse species in as many hostile environments as the Doctor has, it's no surprise that s/he has a pretty good idea of how to get the better of people.

Obi-Wan Kenobi

Like Doctor Who, Obi-Wan Kenobi is a figure from fantasy/sci-fi, but his power manifests itself in a different way. Where the Doctor is mercurial, Kenobi is calm and enigmatic. He provides a space of absolute security for Luke Skywalker, being a mentor and father figure whose wisdom has a strong element of spirituality. At the same time, he has extraordinary power as a warrior. As originally conceived, he was modelled on Gandalf from JRR Tolkien's *The Lord of the Rings*.

Wendy Rhoades

The first series of *Billions*, in which Wendy Rhoades is a supporting character, premiered in January 2016. It's set in the heady world of financial wheeler dealing and Rhoades is the psychiatrist turned performance coach working for the hero yet married to the attorney investigating the hero's complex – and possibly dodgy – business practices. Wealthy and powerful in her own right, Rhoades has been instrumental in helping the hero grow his company.

In the context of the series, she embodies the feminine principle.[8] She understands what motivates everyone in the organisation and is therefore able to nurture them, addressing the realities they face rather than participating in the office gameplay. She is not on the board or in the leadership team; rather she works constantly in the background: wandering the organisation and meeting staff at all levels, finding out what is really going on, integrating information and influencing the system. Her motivational insights are so popular that they can be found all over the internet.

Vesemir

A key figure in the video game *The Witcher 3: Wild Hunt*, Vesemir is the *éminence grise* at Kaer Morhen, the thirteenth-century keep where witchers (monster slayers who have undergone rigorous physical, mental and spiritual preparations for their role) of the School of the Wolf are trained. He is mentor to the legendary Geralt, greatest witcher of them all.

---

8   The feminine principle or archetype is the aspect of the self that is associated with creation, healing, intuition, feeling, the unconscious and collaboration. It is not necessarily related to gender but is a quality of energy that may be present in all beings.

It's clear that the Mighty Advisor has been there all along in our collective consciousness, a distinctive presence in mythology and folk tales and endlessly reworked in the contemporary fictions on screens and in books. These figures share characteristic traits, such as their charisma and wide-ranging knowledge, and we can easily recognise them and their function in all sorts of narratives.

But what about in real life? In the next chapter, we'll examine how these *éminences grises* have operated throughout history and what their role is in the modern world.

2 The Mighty Advisor
delights in using their
catalytic energy to
keep an organisation
slightly off-balance,
so that new vistas and
directions open up.

CHAPTER 2

Mighty Advisors Old And New

In fiction and mythology, we can endow heroes, villains and bit players with any characteristics we want. Real life is not so obliging, so do the non-fiction counterparts of our archetypes, past and present, live up to the roles we attribute to them?

Real-world Mighty Advisors, as we'll discover, display archetypal qualities some or all of the time, while manifesting extreme individuality. Their presence has endured from the Stone Age through to the Digital Age and it would be no exaggeration to say that many of them have changed the course of history.

Mighty Advisors throughout history

The examples I've chosen cover approximately 500 years and bring us up to the beginning of the last century. The individuals themselves have operated in widely differing cultures, but all, to some degree, in a political context.

It's worth noting that the disciplines that influenced these historical figures were of their time. The earliest of them had a strong religious faith and a grounding in philosophy rooted in a classical education. Only as we move towards our own time do we find psychology becoming an explicit area of knowledge for Mighty Advisors – though it was accepted that their forebears had the perspicacity to see into people's hearts and minds.

John Dee (1527–1608/9)

My first encounter with John Dee was when I walked into the large building on Euston Road in London owned by the Wellcome Trust, a charitable foundation that supports health research. Here, in this temple of science, hung a Victorian portrait of the man known as 'the Queen's conjuror' standing in front of Elizabeth I and her assembled court, performing some kind of alchemical experiment. Both the painting and the man contained mysterious secrets: the painting originally showed Dee standing inside a circle of skulls, but these have been painted over.

Dee was a mathematician, natural scientist and practitioner of esoteric arts. His personal library, the most comprehensive in England at the time, totalled over 4,000 volumes, all of which he is believed to have read. He claimed that he could talk to angels and possessed a crystal ball and a magic mirror made of obsidian, which he used for 'scrying'– peering into the future. At the same time, he made close observations of the weather and invented a code with which to record them.

John Dee Performing an Experiment Before Queen Elizabeth I,
oil painting by Henry Gillard Glindoni (1852–1913)

As advisor to Queen Elizabeth, he advocated establishing colonies in the New World and provided technical support for the voyages of discovery that would make this possible. He has been credited with coining the term 'British Empire' and is said to have been the model for the magician Prospero in Shakespeare's *The Tempest.* The experimental research laboratory that he set up at his home in Mortlake can be seen as the forerunner of the current nexus between professional science and financial interests.

François Leclerc du Tremblay (1577–1638)

As the inspiration for the term *éminence grise*, Father Joseph invites further scrutiny. Again, there is a portrait painted centuries after his death that sums up his compelling aura – see the page before the introduction. On a grand staircase bedecked with a tapestry bearing the royal coat of arms, a group of splendidly dressed noblemen bow deeply to a figure passing them on the stairs. Simply dressed in a grey cloak, he is engrossed in a small book and does not notice them. Despite his age, there is a lightness to his presence. The painting projects both the humility and reverence the courtiers feel and a sense that this apparently still moment is pregnant with excitement.

As the confidant of Cardinal Richelieu, Father Joseph found himself at the heart of power in seventeenth century France and instrumental to the diplomacy of the Thirty Years' War. Aldous Huxley's biography of Father Joseph provides a flavour of the man's methods: '... occasionally, too, he permitted himself an outburst of blunt frankness, such as a gentleman may be excused for giving vent to when speaking to his equals. Then, suddenly, the tone would change again, and he was once more the visionary friar, licensed by his habit to denounce wrongdoing even in the highest place, to give warnings even to princes of its fatal consequences in this world and the next.'[9]

When Richelieu, despite his power and status, felt disheartened at the scale of the political projects he was embroiled in, it was Father Joseph's determination that carried him through, and Richelieu felt the lack of support keenly when Father Joseph died.

Goethe (1749–1832)

Johann Wolfgang von Goethe is described in his Wikipedia entry as a poet, playwright, novelist, scientist, statesman, theatre director, critic and amateur artist – if he's not a polymath, I don't know who is.

As a giant of European literature, he is perhaps best known for his first novel, *The Sorrows of Young Werther*, and his epic play, *Faust*. In 1788, he published his first major scientific work, *The Metamorphosis of Plants*; three years later, he became managing director of the theatre at Weimar. He had already been a member of the Duke of Saxe-Weimar's privy council, in which

---

9   A Huxley, *Grey Eminence*

role he had supervised the reopening of silver mines, brought in reforms at the University of Jena and contributed to the redevelopment of the ducal palace and park.

Goethe's influence has perhaps been the most diffuse of all the exemplars we have looked at so far, in that it was not directed at one individual. The philosophers Hegel, Schopenhauer, Kierkegaard and Nietzsche were all inspired by him, as were the composers Mozart and Mahler. Much later, electrical engineer Nikola Tesla would have the brainwave that led to his discovery of alternating current while reciting a verse from *Faust*, as he recalled in an article in *Scientific American* in 1915.[10] It was Rudolf Steiner's article on Goethe's fairy tale *The Green Snake and the Beautiful Lily*, and the potential for personal transformation it represented, that led to Steiner being invited to join the Theosophical Society, with lasting consequences for children's education.

Helena Blavatsky (1831–1891)

That same Theosophical Society, described as 'a very wide umbrella, under which quite a few things could find a place',[11] was co-founded in 1875 by Helena Blavatsky. Another individual with a diffuse legacy In terms of archetypes, she clearly represents the wanderer and, to a degree, the shaman able to access a spiritual world. She claimed to have travelled extensively

10   N Tesla, 'Some personal recollections'
11   G Lachman, *Madame Blavatsky*

in Europe, the Americas and India, and to have met spiritual adepts from whom she received training that enabled her to synthesise religion, philosophy and science.

In 1877 Blavatsky published *Isis Unveiled*,[12] the work that summed up her world view and brought together discrete ideas that had not until then been linked, as she attempted to reconcile contemporary advances in science, such as Darwin's theory of evolution, with occultism. She was a controversial figure throughout her life and critics doubted her claims about her travels and her capacities as a medium, but her work introduced many to Hindu and Buddhist philosophy and influenced the development of the New Age movement.

Rasputin (1869–1916)

Finally, no consideration of Mighty Advisors throughout history would be complete without mention of Rasputin, the Russian monk who was at the side of Tsar Nicholas for ten years before he was assassinated by those who mistrusted his influence over the royal family.

Rasputin was born a peasant and underwent a religious conversion during a visit to a monastery in 1897. In the years that followed, he made many more pilgrimages and began to develop a small following, which eventually resulted in his introduction to St Petersburg society. In 1905, he met the tsar, and it was

---

12   HP Blavatsky, *Isis Unveiled*

not long before the tsar and tsarina became convinced that Rasputin had the power to heal their son Alexei, who suffered from haemophilia. Nobody quite knows how he did it, but Rasputin was able to control Alexei's bleeding and so, not surprisingly, he became a fixture in the royal household. Inevitably, there were those who resented him, and rumours of his unorthodox practices abounded. Finally his detractors felt that his relationship with the tsarina had become inappropriate and made him the scapegoat for Russia's economic decline. Assassinating Rasputin proved difficult, though: massive doses of poison apparently failed to have any effect and he was still able to turn on his attackers after a gunshot wound to the chest – it would take two further shots to despatch him.[13]

Not a model ending for a Mighty Advisor, to say the least. We'll look at how things can go wrong for Mighty Advisors in the next section.

The modern advisor

Career paths are far more clear-cut in the modern era, and education and training serve to sort people into silos, refining and deepening their knowledge and skills in one area rather than broadening them out. It's hard, then, to imagine a job description for a Mighty Advisor – and you will never see that title printed on anyone's business card. Yet despite all the

---

13   D Smith, *Rasputin*

obstacles the regimentation of a contemporary workplace puts in their way, there are still people who find themselves in this position – and I think 'find themselves' is the right choice of words here: none of the historical figures we've looked at set out to occupy the role they ended up in. So how and why do certain people elude the formal posts and titles most of us are expected to take up, and become the enigmatic characters we've been exploring? We'll look at what sets Mighty Advisors apart in the modern workplace and consider a couple of examples of them in action.

WORKING ON THE WIRING

It's important to recognise the ways in which certain people's minds are wired. In my work with CEOs I've seen how focused they are, which of course is a good thing. I often give them a blank sheet of paper to throw all the parts of their strategy onto and tell them that their only boundary is the edge of the paper. What I find, though, is that some of them cannot see the patterns and the forces – what I call The Game – surrounding them.

I recall a conversation with a chief officer in the biotech industry who kept asking me about separate elements of his business: 'How would I work with pharma on this? How can I build manufacturing to respond to that demand?'

As I often do, I wondered whether these questions were coming from naïvety and lack of experience, or from an inability to perceive that these elements were cogs in a wider system.

I couldn't get hold of where he was coming from. I wanted to ask him, 'What's on your chessboard? What do the individual pieces represent? Who are the masters of this game? Is this your question or are you asking me in case your boss is getting it wrong?'

Therapeutics usually take a long time to develop, often as long as seven years, and of course the life of the patent then extends for many years beyond that. That whole stretch of time must be scrutinised closely, as the pitfalls of tomorrow lie in the actions of today.

I have to understand more of the context, the 'why'. If I can't see everything, I sense that something is missing. Once I can see all the moving parts and understand the overall nature of the game, I can begin to provide answers – or at least start to ask more of the big questions.

Those who have an all-encompassing overview, or who sense a 'deep structure' within and between systems, are drawn to this type of work. Although people I've worked with in the past have sometimes said to me, 'You have a mind the size of a planet' (and who wouldn't love a compliment like that?) I maintain it's more to do with how I see things than the sum of my knowledge. When confronted with a problem, I like to look at it from as high a vantage point as I can.

Mighty Advisors are not usually motivated by money or status, because The Game is intrinsically rewarding. They delight in using their catalytic energy to keep an organisation slightly off-balance, so that new vistas and directions open up.

Leaders carry the can for the highs and lows of their organisation, which can sap their energy. It's the job of the Mighty Advisor to make up that deficit and to maintain the energy of the organisation. At times, it's almost as if the leader and the Mighty Advisor are opposing forces; it's the energy that this generates that moves the organisation forward.

More than a coach

There is a wide range of expertise available for the CEO, but in a fragmented format that seems to have been pre-defined by the MBA-type approach. You can hire a coach, a transaction advisor, an HR expert – the list goes on. A coach is an individual the leader can work with closely to examine their personal needs and refine their goals, but the coaching remit stops there.

It's true that some of the techniques deployed by some *éminences grises*, both now and in the past, are used by coaches: the positive psychology, the confidence building and the emphasis on the importance of visualising one's aspirations. But the Mighty Advisor, let's not forget, is a chameleon: sometimes as supportive and encouraging as a personal coach; sometimes the most devilish of devil's advocates; sometimes the most stimulating of interlocutors, prompting you towards insights you didn't know you were capable of.

It's no coincidence that many of the people brought in as Mighty Advisors in the modern era come from marketing or advertising backgrounds. Not only are they looking at the presentation of an issue, but they are constantly monitoring its reception. Alastair Campbell is an obvious example of this approach: his insistence that the Labour Party remain on message at all times was crucial in helping them win three terms in office. The synergy between Campbell and Labour Party leader Tony Blair simply worked, and it was only when the cohesiveness within the party began to fray that the New Labour project foundered.

Uncluttered by responsibilities

As a leader, it can be hard to avoid political entrapment. Particularly in a large organisation, there are factions and forces in play that require careful negotiation, another claim on the leader's bandwidth. None of this is any concern of the Mighty Advisor, leaving them free to take in the big picture without any distraction. Big data is the key to so much understanding that it's not surprising that tech companies, with their habit of systems thinking, have come to dominate in the way they do.

This does not mean, however, that the Mighty Advisor has no responsibility. I would not class Machiavelli as a Mighty Advisor, despite his insights. The cynicism and ruthlessness of his advice contains no redeeming qualities, and his insistence that the end justifies the means has scope to ignore suffering. The Mighty Advisor's all-encompassing view should act as a defence against negative manipulations. The truly Mighty Advisor would disengage from any advice that ultimately threatened their organisation or the wider community and would not act primarily in their own interest. Where we have seen Mighty Advisors face difficulty, it's because their mission has become corrupted: they've begun to abuse their power to serve their own ends. Rasputin weakened his position when he began on the path of self-aggrandisement, abusing his privileged position in the royal household by accepting bribes and sexual favours from those in thrall to his charisma.[14]

In our own time, Dominic Cummings is a classic example of this same phenomenon. Whatever you think of the Brexit project, he successfully masterminded the Leave campaign and propelled Boris Johnson to victory in the 2019 General Election. His big mistake was flouting lockdown guidelines by fleeing to Durham.[15] He

---

14   D Smith, *Rasputin*
15   Reality Check Team, 'Dominic Cummings'

undermined faith in public health legislation enacted by the government and paid dearly for it. We'll examine his role and his trajectory as a Mighty Advisor more closely in the next chapter.

Jonathan Van-Tam

In stark contrast, the UK's Deputy Chief Medical Officer is a public figure who you could say had a 'good' pandemic. He emerged as the relatable face of community health messaging, able to translate the complex epidemiological information he needed to get across into language and concepts that the average viewer or listener could understand. As a natural storyteller, he made effective use of metaphor (see Chapter 6) and even in the teeth of a frightening plague managed to make people feel a bit better about themselves and the future. His personal warmth and his quirky, pilot-style use of the term 'over' in his Zoom calls stood out from the more sober delivery styles of his colleagues. Such was his popularity that you could buy T-shirts bearing his image, with the legend, 'In J Van-Tam we trust'.

Valerie Jarrett

Valerie Jarrett, a psychology graduate who went on to study law, was a senior advisor to President Obama from 2009 to 2017, responsible for public engagement and intergovernmental affairs, urban affairs, women and girls, and sport. It was when she was deputy chief of staff to Mayor Richard Daley of Chicago that she hired Michelle Robinson, then engaged to Barack Obama. It was the start of a lasting friendship between Jarrett and the Obamas with, in its earliest phase, Jarrett taking both under her wing.

Michelle Obama has described her as somebody who automatically understands someone's values and is never afraid to tell you the truth. 'She knows the buttons, the soft spots, the history, the context.'[16] She was the perfect fit for a highly intelligent president whose natural tendency was to stand somewhat apart from the people he was governing; her role was to act as the bridge between the voices inside the White House and those outside. During Obama's time in office, Jarrett is credited with helping him gain the trust of black voters and mending fences with the Clintonite wing of the Democratic Party, not to mention talking him through some of the major decisions he had to make. Given her friendship with the Obamas, her official presence as an advisor in the White House was sometimes viewed as controversial, but in practice there do not seem to have been any conflicts of interest. In fact, she seems to have been the epitome of soft power in action.

I have had no shortage of candidates to choose from in selecting real-world examples of Mighty Advisors who reflect age-old archetypes. Their subtle and wide-ranging talents are as relevant as ever in the modern world, and I'd go so far

---

16　J Kantor, 'An old hometown mentor, still at Obama's side'

as to say that they will be the last to lose their jobs to robots – even allowing for the fact that we now have examples of cybertherapists.

As we've seen, eccentricity is a key feature of these individuals, and they have defied the persistent call of the workplace to conform. In the next chapter, we'll examine why this is such a powerful trait.

3 The thought disruptor
is like the grit
introduced into an
oyster: in time, the
oyster will produce
a pearl.

CHAPTER 3

Eccentrics

We have become an increasingly individualistic society, yet conformity reigns supreme. Received wisdom, groupthink and, in a business context, the MBA playbook, are default positions that we adopt too readily and at our peril. If you need evidence for this, think no further than the small number of voices warning about the financial crash of 2008; they were viewed as eccentrics, but they were vindicated.

Eccentricity literally means 'out of the centre'. In this chapter, I'll be looking more closely at how a Mighty Advisor deploys this characteristic – perhaps consciously and deliberately, perhaps not – to influence others.

Out of the circle

As Groucho Marx purportedly said, 'I don't want to belong to any club that would have me as a member.'[17] His manufactured outrage was directed at any organisation that would admit someone as reprehensible as himself within their walls, but for me the gag captures the disruptive energy of the eccentric – who is entirely 'unclubbable'.

---

17   A Marx, *My Life with Groucho*

The Marx Brothers' films are one long paean to the creative possibilities of disruption and the liberating humour of seeing the po-faced and strait-laced confronted with the anarchic and unpredictable.

Such oddness has undeniable power – it stops people in their tracks. They begin asking, 'Who *is* that person? What are they doing? Where are they going with this?' This is how the eccentric disarms startled observers: they become so engrossed – mesmerised even – by this individual's antics that their own agendas and expectations are suspended.

There are many types and examples of eccentrics who can come to occupy the role of Mighty Advisor; here, I introduce you to some who you might recognise.

The jester

Speaking truth unto power is a hazardous pursuit, as many a whistle-blower can testify to, but when these words originate not from righteous anger but from someone who seems frankly unhinged, they are far more palatable. This is the function of the court jester, who is able to say things to the monarch's face that other courtiers would hesitate to whisper in the palace corridor.

The Fool in Shakespeare's *King Lear* is a prime example of this. All those around King Lear know that he has made a serious mistake in dividing his kingdom between his two most ambitious daughters and turning his back on the most loving one – because she spoke the truth rather than flattering him. Any attempt to reason with Lear, to get him to modify his erratic and self-destructive behaviour, is met with towering rages.

'Thou hadst little wit in thy bald crown when thou gavest thy golden one away,'[18] declares the Fool – and gets away with it. He remains the trusted confidant by the king's side, his mad wisdom offsetting the king's growing folly. He enjoys a licence to speak his mind not only because of his role as fool, but because he is outside the hierarchy of the court. Coming from someone of higher rank, his criticism would be unacceptable.

As with many of the Mighty Advisors we've looked at so far, the Fool is bound to Lear by unshakeable loyalty, unhesitatingly going with him into the storm when Lear is banished from his daughter's castle.

The expert

The expert is set apart by virtue of their specialist knowledge. Whereas in times gone by this might have been knowledge of alchemy and the dark arts, now it is likely to be a rarefied scientific knowledge.

After a few years in the doldrums (summed up by Michael Gove: 'I think the people of this

---

18   G Taylor et al, *The New Oxford Shakespeare*

country have had enough of experts'[19]) their popularity has come roaring back, especially epidemiologists, virologists, vaccinologists and the like. The Covid-19 pandemic showed that there are times when we must place our faith in experts. The acknowledged expert who has demonstrated that their learning, experience and understanding underpin wise decisions is valued, and often given carte blanche to problem-solve as they see fit, even though their approach might be unorthodox.

SCIENTIST OR SAVANT?

I've never allowed my training as a scientist to get in the way of listening to my intuition, but it took me some time to feel comfortable with revealing this publicly.

Many times I've followed a hunch that a particular drug would be worth developing. I wasn't that bothered about the logic of the business case; I simply had a deep belief that there was both a medical need and a public demand for a specific treatment. This was what drove my willingness to continue to work on developing the drug without being held up by gathering interim commercial or scientific evidence.

19   R Portes, 'Who needs experts?'

What enables an expert to be truly effective as a Mighty Advisor is an ability to see their own specialism in a wider context and predict how the two will interact. It is a bonus if that expert also has well-developed communication skills, as in the case of Jonathan Van-Tam, whose role during the pandemic we looked at in the last chapter.

The data cruncher: Frederick Lindemann

Physicist Frederick Lindemann was Churchill's chief scientific advisor and closest confidant throughout the war. A controversial and arrogant figure, 'The Prof' alienated many of his colleagues, but no one could fault his commitment to the prime minister. More endearing evidence of his eccentricity was his habit of heading off to fly a plane wearing a bowler hat and clutching an umbrella.

His most significant contribution to the war efforts was the establishment of 'S-Branch', a unit made up of subject specialists tasked with scrutinising and aggregating data from government ministries, producing succinct charts to illuminate every aspect of the conduct of the war. They were, in effect, the forerunners of today's data and information analysts.

As a leader, Churchill did not want to be swamped with data; S-Branch's presentations told him what he needed to know, when he needed to know it. Their compelling summations, for example, comparing the tonnage of German bombs dropped on Britain with the tonnage of British bombs dropped on Germany, enabled him to make rapid decisions based on sound data, and had a direct impact on the war effort.

Like so many other Mighty Advisors, Lindemann, despite his impressive scientific credentials, did not confine himself to his specialist subject. General Ismay, Churchill's chief military assistant during the war, described Lindemann's activities thus: 'He would write a memorandum on high strategy one day, and a thesis on egg production on the next.'[20]

The maverick: Sherlock Holmes

Sherlock Holmes is one of those fictional characters who has taken on a life of his own, even down to having a real London address. He is a very particular man, in the Italian sense of the word – *particolare*, meaning individual, different from the general run of men. Highlighting Holmes's difference is the man he has at his side, Dr John Watson, a solid, conventional figure, to serve as his foil.

Sherlock Holmes's methods combine science with more unpredictable practices. He is knowledgeable about chemistry and many of his investigations entail what we would now call forensic science, for example, analysis of footprints and fingerprints, and toxicology tests. His powers of observation are second to none and he does not limit their application to inanimate objects; he is also skilled at reading moods, fleeting expressions and body language.

---

20   A Fort, *Prof*

When it comes to unravelling a problem, he often requires complete solitude, retreating deep inside his head to discern the patterns that all the data from his investigations add up to. Often, he won't eat, as he believes that starvation refines the faculties.

Holmes's love of showmanship serves him well when a disguise is called for and there's no denying he enjoys the drama of the great reveal, presenting the fruits of his astounding feats of detection to an admiring public.

Not surprisingly, Holmes's creator, Sir Arthur Conan Doyle, shares some of his character's attributes. A medical doctor whose experiences at a Jesuit boarding school had left him a confirmed agnostic, in later life he became interested in spiritualism. His belief in the supernatural even led him to accept as genuine photographs of fairies that were later proven to be fakes.

Holmes is surely the blueprint for every troubled and moody loner detective who has appeared in print or on our screens since. (Now, the truly innovative screen detective would be a happily married teetotaller who is a stickler for following procedures yet still manages to get results!)

Inside the circle

The Mighty Advisor should avoid being drawn into the inner circle, as it's often a recipe for disaster – for the advisor, at any rate. As soon as they step inside that circle, their wings are clipped, and they will be subject to the constraints of the organisation's rules and customs.

The chief of staff role, for example, is very different from that of Mighty Advisor. The chief of staff is responsible for executing the will of the leader; the Mighty Advisor is the influencer and should maintain the distinction between influence and power. When Mighty Advisors give way to their egos, it generates a competitive rather than a creative tension with the leader; in this scenario, the Mighty Advisor does not survive.

A cautionary tale: Dominic Cummings

What initially aroused my curiosity about Conservative Party special advisor Dominic Cummings when his role at the heart of the Brexit project began to emerge, was his website.[21] Far more interesting than what was written about him in the papers were the topics that he wrote about on this site. It was clear that he was exploring, among other things, systems thinking, the potential of polemics to shift the agenda and the constructive challenge of 'oddness' itself – hence his later attempt to recruit 'weirdos' to the Cabinet Office.

In the popular view, Cummings's wardrobe was every bit as noteworthy as his fiendish success in navigating the Vote Leave campaign to a successful conclusion.[22] Surrounded by

21 https://dominiccummings.com
22 HJ Parkinson, 'Canvas of lies'

regulation suits, sober ties and crisp shirts, Cummings stood out a mile in his beanie, sweatshirts and jogging pants, leaving the beholder to guess at how much of this was because he liked to be comfortable and how much was to do with cocking a snook at authority.

The Dominic Cummings story demonstrates perfectly that Mighty Advisors perform best in an eccentric role, outside the circle. It was when Cummings was brought right into the centre of the circle as Boris Johnson's chief of staff that things began to go wrong. Invested with the power to hire and fire on behalf of the government he seems to have used it unwisely, not following the correct dismissal procedures. What's more, his position near the top of the formal hierarchy, seeking to manipulate the fate of ministers, made him more susceptible to the enmity of members of the government. Some of the guerrilla tactics you can get away with in a campaigning organisation are simply not appropriate in a publicly funded organisation. It was inevitable, after his flouting of the lockdown regulations, that sooner or later he would have to go.

Eccentrics in practice

How can leaders and organisations best work with Mighty Advisors? They need to have a constructive relationship, but one that doesn't compromise their independence. The best approach is to have clear mechanisms enabling the advisor to contribute drawing from the widest scope of their practice yet maintain sufficient distance to do so freely and dispassionately.

'Practice' is a word that encompasses a range of meanings, all of which are relevant to the Mighty Advisor. There is the suggestion of rehearsing or repeating something to become perfect at it, which describes the way in which they both deepen and broaden their knowledge and experience. An artist's way of working is often described as their practice, denoting a highly individual and creative output with meaning and cultural impact. Crucially, the word also signals action – making an impact in the real world, which should be the end goal of the Mighty Advisor's input.

Thought leadership

Much as I detest organisational jargon, it's hard to argue with the usefulness of the phrase 'thinking outside the box'. Changing and unpredictable times demand new thinking, and the leader, however energetic and effective, is not always the best person to supply it. Most companies could do with either a department of thought leadership or a board of thought leaders to be a pipeline feeding new ideas into the organisation, as everyone else is likely to be too bogged down in running the business.

Political parties often have satellite groups composed of people who don't have any departmental or ministerial obligations who are therefore free to float ideas and stimulate policy, such as the Fabian Society for the Labour Party and the Bow Group for the

Conservative Party, not to mention a host of thinktanks with varying degrees of influence. Their effectiveness is patchy, though, not least because of the range of motivations behind their existence. Some are no more than lobby groups with an axe to grind and generous corporate funding doled out in self-interest.

Genuine thought leadership resides not with those looking at a problem from the inside, working with a known set of parameters to achieve what may be a fairly limited objective, but with those who are open-minded about what the problem is, drawing on the widest possible frame of reference to formulate it and to explore the solutions. This is the scope of the task that the Mighty Advisor should be offered.

Thought disruption

Edward de Bono is one of the most high-profile of thought disrupters. Again, he is something of a polymath: he is a medical doctor, but is also qualified in psychiatry, has been nominated for a Nobel Prize in Economics, and is Professor of Thinking at the University of Advancing Technology in Arizona. Many people will be familiar with his Thinking Hats methodology, which invites you to think about a problem from six different perspectives.[23] It is a favourite tool of mine – so much so that you will find on my website a video of me wearing six daft hats in tribute to him.

23   E De Bono, *Six Thinking Hats*

De Bono's other contribution to disruptive thinking is the concept of Po, or lateral thinking. The word 'Po', intended to suggest forward movement in thinking, represents the syllable 'po' from words such as **po**etry, hy**po**thesis, sup**po**se and **po**ssible as well as the first two letters of '**p**rovoking **o**peration'.[24] Po can generate a multitude of ideas, some of which will be frankly silly, but they enable thinking to move on from entrenched ideas to innovation. A presentation by Edward de Bono is startlingly different from a standard PowerPoint presentation. He favours antiquated overhead projector technology, because this gives him the freedom to write directly on the slides with coloured felt tips, meaning there are no limits to his flow or to his creativity.

My business card has 'thought disrupter' on it, because I don't want anyone to be in any doubt. If they invite me to a meeting, that's what they're going to get. When the same cast of characters meets regularly, it's inevitable that their thinking will get stale. Most people think they know what they are doing, and much of the time they will be violently agreeing with one another. I often stay quiet in a meeting, formulating exactly what I want to say. When I speak, it will be to ask a question that is big and different. I want to get to the essence of the conversation and say something that will make the group look at their project in a different way.

---

24 E De Bono, *Po*

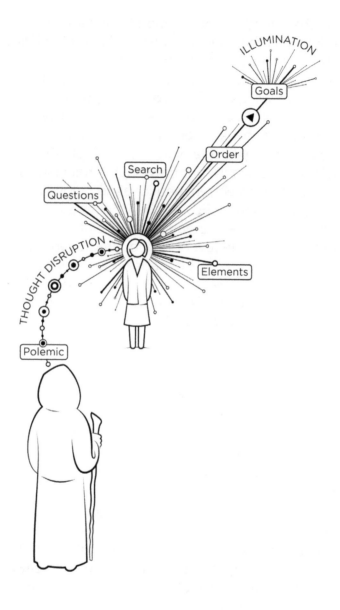

ILLUMINATION

Goals

Order

Search

Questions

THOUGHT DISRUPTION

Elements

Polemic

*Thought disruption taking leaders on
a journey of illumination*

The thought disruptor is like the grit introduced into an oyster: in time, the oyster will produce a pearl.

STIRRING

I see it as my duty to ask awkward questions. It's the only way to get over groupthink. I will often go into a company and challenge the received wisdom about their products. Through probing who, for example, benefits from a specific drug, I'm able to arrive at the Achilles' heel of their processes or their market. Once I've found it, I know where I'm going.

This approach has served me well when I've been advising on investment, as it goes way beyond what most people do in the way of due diligence. Anyone can look at the balance sheets for past years, but it's only by penetrating beyond the façade to the information that people might prefer you not to know that you can bring the real picture into focus and unsettle leaders enough to provoke them into action.

High-functioning people are complex, and it can take a lot of acquired skill and energy to find out what is going on. Often, I simply persist in saying I don't understand something, to urge them towards greater levels of clarity.

If I'm asked to join a board, I'll do it willingly, but they can't expect me to be 'one of them'. That's not what I'm there for. I'm there to build a completely different view of what is going on in the organisation, to see the whole framework of their activity via an aerial view – and to reverse their thinking about it, if that's what's needed.

Eccentrics in an organisation

Sometimes it becomes clear that individuals working within an organisation are exceeding the boundaries of their organisation. They're proving hard to pigeonhole; they don't seem to belong in any department. You can't work out what level of the hierarchy they sit within, and yet, their contribution is extremely valuable; you wouldn't want to lose it. Such people often end up given being a vague title and a licence to roam, as long as they bring back intelligence, the undercurrent of trends and opinions, to inform the direction of the organisation.

By way of example, let's consider journalist and broadcaster Janet Street Porter. A flamboyant personality with a broad cockney accent, she has consistently been ahead of trends in popular culture. She was a controversial head of BBC2's youth and entertainment programmes, and in 2000 she was nominated for the Mae West Award for Most Outspoken Woman in the Industry. She became editor of *The Independent on Sunday* in 1999 and increased the paper's circulation by nearly 12%,[25] but then

---

25   T Vahimagi, 'Street-Porter, Janet (1946–)'

took a step back to become editor at large in 2002, with a remit to roam far and wide. She has never toned herself down at anyone's behest, and whenever I come across her while channel hopping, I can be sure that she will be taking the contrarian view.

In Chapter 7, we'll explore how organisations can identify such individuals in their midst and ensure they create the conditions for them to thrive and give their best.

Call them what you will – eccentrics, *éminences grises*, square pegs in round holes – these oddball characters are an essential aid for a leader and often the lifeblood of organisations. They combine a depth of knowledge and expertise, recognition of unseen currents and an ability to map all this onto a grand canvas. In the next chapter, we'll look at exactly what constitutes the knowledge that gives these individuals their authority.

4 The Mighty Advisor
has the distinctive
talent of being able
to combine logic with
an acceptance of
the workings of the
subconscious mind.

CHAPTER 4

What Is Wisdom?

Wisdom is the most basic weapon in the Mighty Advisor's armoury. It can be hard to pin down, and I suspect there is little consensus on how to define it. A vox pop on the subject would probably produce answers such as experience, understanding of a body of knowledge, judgement and intuition.

Doxa

The word I favour for this wisdom is 'doxa', as it encompasses all these elements and more, which is why it is the bedrock of what the Mighty Advisor has to offer. In the original Greek, 'doxa' means a shared belief. Shared understanding is vital for a society or organisation to function effectively, so the Mighty Advisor's wisdom must be embedded in this deep knowledge, whatever you call it. Anyone with a comprehension of the doxa within which they are working, whether in an organisation or in the wider world, has the key to 'holding the ring' for the group. A strong doxa gives a group a competitive advantage.

As the repository of this collective and all-embracing wisdom, Mighty Advisors guarantee a degree of stability amid change. This direct connection with the doxa is also the source of their authenticity – because it cannot be faked. Mighty Advisors will manifest their access to the doxa in many ways, depending on context and their own personal qualities. It is a fluid tool rather than a fixed skill, composed of the elements mentioned above, and more, in different ratios, which the Mighty Advisor deploys in a bespoke fashion to answer a specific need.

Let's look in detail at the components of the Mighty Advisor's wisdom, and challenge some of the assumptions about them.

Experience

The more experience you have, the better you can predict what may happen next in a given situation, the more aware you will be of possible pitfalls and the more confident you will be in your suggested solutions. Experience enables you to slow down a situation, take a measured view, and make a judgement that takes into account the widest possible ramifications.

Fictional Mighty Advisors have often lived through many generations, acquiring experience and knowledge far beyond the scope of mortals, and many real-life examples have a longevity and durability that makes them irreplaceable – think David Attenborough. You also need to consider the quality of experience. There is a tremendous difference between someone who has simply done their job twenty times or over twenty years and one who has who amassed twenty years' worth of cumulative knowledge and experience, adapting and innovating along the way.

And yet there are people who seem to be able to bypass the actual gathering of experience. These are the people we often describe as having an 'old head on young shoulders', or as being a 'wise child'. They seem to have been born with a deeper understanding and intuition, giving them a different perspective from others.

Intuition

Experience offers more than just the opportunity for pattern recognition and prediction based on past events. It becomes transmuted into what I call 'embodied intuition': an ability to sense subtle connections, influences and consequences. In his book *Blink*, Malcom Gladwell characterises intuition as being made up of infinitesimal recognitions that we are not conscious of. In this way, it's a form of unconscious competence, which in psychology refers to a skill that has been mastered so completely that that the individual is not even aware of deploying it. The Mighty Advisor may not be aware of having acquired this embodied intuition and certainly will have done so spontaneously rather than deliberately. It's the mental equivalent of muscle memory.

As twentieth century philosopher Christian de Quincey observed, 'We are continually sharing messages with the world around us, picking them up in our body-mind, processing, metabolising them and expressing them.'[26] A Mighty Advisor has an acutely refined

---

26   C De Quincey, *Deep Spirit*

sensitivity to the systems in their environment, both internal and external. Being able to combine logic with an acceptance of the workings of the subconscious mind in this way is a distinctive talent of the Mighty Advisor. The subconscious mind is constantly turning over problems, which means that ideas and solutions may spring spontaneously into the conscious mind, with no awareness of a sequence of thoughts that could have led to them.

Mighty Advisors can see both the whole and all the constituent parts at the same time, and what's on the periphery is as vivid as what's at the centre. They can take uncertainties, ambiguities and complexities in their stride, confident that they will be able to discern the threads to pick up to complete the picture or disentangle the knots that obscure its meaning.

PENETRATING THE LABYRINTH

Some years ago, I was fortunate enough to be taken on by a large French pharma company to recreate their research and development (R&D) organisation. The founder had died recently and it soon became clear to me that he had constructed this organisation as a series of silos. In fact, it reminded me of a neighbourhood pharmacy in which he had arranged all the drugs out the back and all the cosmetics by the door as you came in.

I set about creating a far more integrated and streamlined organisation that entailed changes throughout the group. As a result, I was retained for several years as, in effect, their *éminence grise*, to guide the company through their new terrain, working closely with the R&D director to ensure that his vision for the scientific direction of the company was reflected in wider decision making.

Mighty Advisors often seem to have their own GPS, enabling them to navigate organisations far more successfully than most, with their finger on the pulse of who is doing what, where and when, and who sits at the heart of which circles of influence. If you were able to look at an aerial photo of an organisational gathering, you would see how people gravitate towards each other. Subject experts cluster together; those in friendship groups find one another; those of equal seniority tend to congregate. Some like to be in the centre of the room, holding court; others seek the safety of the sidelines. The Mighty Advisor stands at the periphery because this is the vantage point from which they can scan people's faces, observe relationships and build an understanding of the hidden architecture of the organisation. The place of the Mighty Advisor is outside the system, peering deep into the heart of it.

Seeing the big picture from a different vantage point is the special attribute of a Mighty Advisor

The word I think best sums up the way a Mighty Advisor apprehends a situation or an organisation is 'grok'. This is a term invented by science fiction writer Robert A Heinlein in his 1961 novel *Stranger in a Strange Land.* Its literal meaning is 'to drink', but in its fullest interpretation it means, 'To understand so thoroughly that an observer becomes part of the process of being observed... It means almost everything that we mean by religion, philosophy and science.' [27]

Knowledge

We accept that Mighty Advisors have access to vast bodies of knowledge. This may be formal learning, acquired through universities and research, or it may be informal knowledge, acquired through personal exploration and observation. The two are not mutually exclusive and Mighty Advisors will certainly encompass both types of knowledge.

Becoming an expert in their field and keeping up with developments within it is simply not enough. Mighty Advisors are characterised by an insatiable curiosity that leads them down many paths, sometimes to unexpected destinations. They refuse to view knowledge in silos, to be pigeonholed as an expert in a single discipline. For the perfect example, look no further than Goethe: a commissioner for mines and highways *and* a dramatist *and* a physicist *and...* But it's thanks to this curiosity that Mighty

---

27   RA Heinlein, *Stranger in a Strange Land*

Advisors are able to make vital connections beyond their nominal area of expertise and foresee the consequences of any given course of action.

Although Mighty Advisors may sometimes retreat into absent-minded professor mode to think deeply about an issue, they never lose sight of the real world. Their knowledge does not exist in a vacuum, and they can share it successfully because they understand how others apprehend reality. Again, I'm drawn to Jonathan Van-Tam as an example of this. As you'd expect of a deputy chief medical officer, he has a doctorate and is a fellow of various professional bodies: FFPH, FRCPath, FFPM, FRSPH, and FRSPB.[28] Yet he still understands life as it is lived by most people. Hence his explanation of the challenges of storing and distributing the Pfizer Covid vaccine: 'This is a complex product with a very fragile cold chain. It's not a yoghurt that can be taken out of the fridge and put back multiple times.'[29]

The knowledge possessed by Mighty Advisors is never knowledge for its own sake, or for show. It's comprehensive, practical and adaptable.

Integrated thinking

I can often identify a wise person by their response to a complex question. They tend to

---

28   Fellow of the Faculty of Public Health, Fellow of the Royal College of Pathology, Fellow of the Faculty of Public Medicine, Fellow of the Royal Society of Public Health and Fellow of the Royal Society of Biology
29   B Morton, 'Jonathan Van-Tam's best analogies'

start off with a sigh: that tells me that they are processing all of their thinking on the matter and attempting to synthesise it into a reasoned and comprehensive answer. The person who comes out with a ready answer is has probably not given the question enough thought; they will have failed to take into account all the dimensions of it and how these interact.

We're often invited to tackle problems in bite-sized pieces; certainly, the model for technological innovation seems to be to make a series of small, incremental improvements. This has its place and allows for forward momentum rather than paralysis in the face of stubborn obstacles, but the danger is that you may not look at the whole picture for long enough to grasp its intricacies before breaking it down into digestible fragments. It can then be difficult to reassemble the big picture from the discrete pieces in front of you – you need to be able to keep in front of you the lid of the jigsaw box bearing the picture. The Mighty Advisor never loses sight of that lid. They have that ability to refocus their thinking, looking at issues from multiple perspectives, sometimes at magnifications of thousands of times, then pulling back to take in the view from the stratosphere. It follows that they use some creative techniques for synthesising all these perspectives.

Thought experiments

Imagination is a vital tool for the Mighty Advisor. Being able to supplement pragmatic thinking and reasoning based on experience with genuine 'blue-sky' thinking is what sets the Mighty Advisor apart. (I see this as being somewhat different from 'thinking the unthinkable', similar though they sound, because in practice the latter often seems to mean thinking that will have adverse consequences for some groups of people).

In the West, we are said to favour the logical brain. It is a brain that works in categories, dealing with known facts, and proceeding in an orderly, linear fashion. It has served us well – the accepted method for scientific investigation is based on this type of thinking – but it can only take us so far. The logical brain is sometimes described as the reptilian brain, because it is programmed for survival and perceives anything unknown as a possible threat. It is also the brain that is responsible for groupthink.

For imagination to flourish, we need to use our creative brains and ways of thinking that are more like that of a child, or of the 'nutty professor' stereotype. It is holistic and freewheeling, making new connections and bringing the apparently disparate together. Being able to ally the logical brain with the creative brain and see the big picture in this way is a characteristic of many inventors. Nikola Tesla, the electrical engineer instrumental in the creation of alternating current (after whom Elon Musk's electric car is named), combined the mind of a scientist with the flair and disruptive energy of a magician. In his autobiography, he described how he could translate words into pictures that he could see vividly, enabling him to communicate them to others: 'These images were at first very blurred and indistinct and would flit away when I tried to concentrate my attention upon them. They gained in strength and distinctness and finally assumed the concreteness of real things.'[30]

On this basis, he suggested that a thought could be used with an image as an experimental method. He would visualise an invention in minute detail before beginning construction of it, and usually did not sketch it beforehand, but worked from the 'memory' of his visualised image.

Mighty Advisors incorporate into such thought experiments an element of 'mind melding', both gathering in inherent knowledge and intuiting what will best serve the leader. Philosopher Roy Sorensen describes a thought experiment as 'opening an enchanted portal; it has the feel of clairvoyance and so excites awe in some and suspicion in others. The wonder of a thought experiment is a special case of our vague puzzlement about how a question can be answered by merely thinking.'[31]

Visualising

We can see from Tesla's account how important it is for the Mighty Advisor to be able to tap into a vivid and detailed representation of the system, the organisation or the community they aim to serve. The map of the losses

30   N Tesla, *My Inventions*
31   R Sorensen, *Thought Experiments*

of Napoleon's army during the Russian campaign of 1812–13 is a classic example of how compelling such a representation can be. In 1869, Charles Joseph Minard, a French civil engineer who pioneered the use of information graphics, produced a map of the fate of the French army. Minard's chief interest was the plight of the soldiers, so the map does not feature any of Napoleon's decisions. Instead, it shows the number of men, the distance they covered, the temperature, and their location at given dates. The tragedy is immediately visible from the width of the band representing the outward journey compared to its dwindling thinness on the return journey, as the temperatures plummet. You can immediately grasp the implications of such a map for strategic planning.

In the interests of highlighting the contributions of women wherever possible, I should also mention US educator and women's rights activist Emma Hart Willard, whose infographics, created in the 1840s and '50s, brought together developments in various disciplines across time and space to create succinct images to use as teaching aids with her students.

In a more immediately recognisable context, consider how many lives might have been saved if Covid health strategists had had an accurate representation of how connected care homes are with their communities, in terms of the constant flow of visitors and staff in and out of the homes and, in the case of agency staff, their onward trajectory to nurse other vulnerable people. Instead, there seems to have

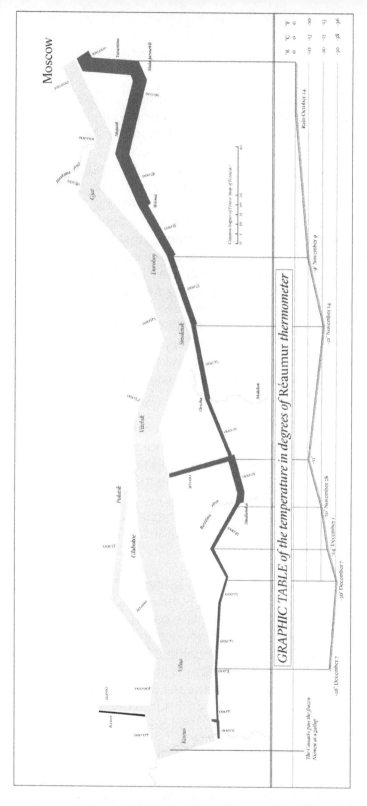

Modern redrawing of Napoleon's 1812 Russian campaign, including a table of degrees in Celsius and Fahrenheit and translated to English

been an assumption that care homes were impermeable bubbles with no mechanism for spreading infection, and that it was therefore safe to send elderly patients back to them from hospitals without any special precautions.

Multiple lenses, three-dimensional thinking, call it what you will – the Mighty Advisor takes a kaleidoscopic approach, in the same way as an architect must produce plans for a building from multiple aspects – side, front and rear elevations, floor plans, cross-sections, etc – before the first stone is laid. Let's not forget that Mr Spock, of course, was skilled in 3D chess.

Sharing wisdom

Mighty Advisors are not the ones in charge, so how do they share their wisdom, ensuring that it's not only understood but acted on by those with the power to bring about change? One way they do this is to ensure that they are using the right channel. Part of their 'metathinking' – their grasp of the big picture – is an understanding of the different ways in which people learn. Choosing the right channel for sharing information is vital. Some leaders will respond to a Mighty Advisor whose style is playful and provoking, others will feel more comfortable with an invitation to reflect on and refine their thinking. Whatever the channel, the aim is the same: to make the penny drop.

Building the chemistry and connection between Mighty Advisor and leader that is required to bring this about is a long process: it can take months, even years. This relationship must be allowed to develop spontaneously; it is far removed from the more transactional relationship a leader might have with a coach, for example, who has been contracted over a short period to facilitate change in a specific area. The role of a potent advisor is embedded in the system, something like the relationship between master and apprentice.

Master and apprentice

The master and apprentice model is well represented in literature. It's based on a relationship that we all understand, being rooted in most cultures. Merlin is the stand-out example from British mythology. He was the mystical figure with the responsibility of preparing the young Arthur for his future role as King of England, passing on his wisdom through journeys of discovery and, finally, by enabling Arthur to draw Excalibur (his sword) from the stone in which it was lodged.

This model has been repeated in countless trades and professions down the ages, and still exists in some areas of work. Apprentices go to work for a master for many years until they have learned all there is to learn. Then they become journeymen, qualified to set up on their own if they wish. Most of these masters would not have been Mighty Advisors, of course, merely people who were good at their jobs and able to pass on their knowledge and expertise. Yet we see their role replicated informally by Mighty Advisors in many contemporary contexts.

Throughout his time as prime minister, Tony Blair had Alastair Campbell by his side in a variety of roles. His reliance on him was not misplaced: Campbell was instrumental in Labour's three successive election victories and Blair has called him a genius. He is also credited with coming up with the phrase 'the People's Princess' upon the death of Princess Diana.

Although he was often resented by the media for his vice-like grip on party and government communications during the Blair years, his modernising approach was effective and out-ward-looking: he opened government briefings to foreign news media, put these briefings themselves on the record and played a key part in the negotiation of the Good Friday Agreement. The Conservative Party in opposi-tion acknowledged that they did not have the means to stop his well-oiled machine.

His work since leaving government bears witness to the breadth of his interests and, interestingly, he too has been appointed an editor at large, for *The New European* newspaper.

The generative process

The ability of the Mighty Advisor to catalyse a leader's thinking is a generative process. The characteristic dialogue of this process has the potential to yield ideas, answers and solutions that individuals working on their own would not arrive at. This approach is therefore transformational in a sense that John Dee, with his knowledge of alchemy, would have understood.

Otto Scharmer, a professor at Massachusetts Institute of Technology, devised what he calls Theory U to formalise a methodology of transformation that helps leaders to move beyond the stale and unproductive behaviours that they may find themselves stuck in.[32] Scharmer has explicitly acknowledged the influence of both Goethe and Rudolf Steiner on his work.

A central feature of Theory U is 'presencing': shedding past patterns, letting go and allowing your inner knowledge to emerge, so as to rebuild through co-creation with others and integrating the activity of heart, head and hand. The shared vision of the future that this process gives rise to allows participants to act with whole ecosystems in mind.

Connectors

Connectedness – to spiritual power, to nature, across time and space – has always been seen as an essential component of wisdom, but perhaps one of its more esoteric elements. Trying to track this connectedness is like trying to ferret out something hidden, whether that's discerning a pattern in big data, observing a subtle phenomenon in the natural world, or trying to pick up the scent of a coming trend.

In *The Tipping Point,* Malcom Gladwell explores the potential of people he calls 'connectors'

---

32   CO Scharmer, *The Essentials of Theory U*

to make ideas come to life and spread them through communities.[33] The connector knows many people in an array of social, professional and cultural circles, and likes to introduce them to one another, creating social architecture and ecosystems. In organisational terms, a Mighty Advisor, through their wandering and with their access all areas, can disseminate ideas far more effectively than top-down messages from the leadership.

We've established that what constitutes the Mighty Advisor's wisdom goes way beyond deep familiarity with a body of knowledge; it lies as much in integrated thinking conducted on the basis of multilayered inquiry and openness to the authentic insights generated by the subconscious. Let's continue our exploration of how Mighty Advisors work to influence leaders and extend their reach beyond the individual.

33   M Gladwell, *The Tipping Point*

5 Though the Mighty Advisor does not have a formal role in a hierarchy, their influence permeates an organisation, or even a nation, bringing about transformation.

CHAPTER 5

Influence

The impact of the true Mighty Advisor goes far beyond having the ear of the leader and guiding them through the challenges they face. It reverberates outwards, opening up the possibilities for change and growth. But how do they accomplish this, in the absence of any levers to pull?

They must have a strong systemic connection with the organisation in question and understand what is appropriate and desirable for the organisation's culture – in effect, they must 'grok' the organisation and the people in it. The aspiration for an organisation to have a clear strategy and follow it through is at constant risk of being undermined, but the Mighty Advisor, with no shareholders bearing down on them or direct push-back from staff, can identify how and where to apply subtle pressure.

Modern marketing

Looking back at advertisements from 100 years ago can be a source of great entertainment. The fashions and the style of illustration are dated, but the crudeness of the messages, the bald exhortations to buy this or that, do just as much to differentiate them from current styles of marketing.

Based on ever more refined segmentation of big data, today's approach to getting inside somebody's head and changing their mindset is far more nuanced. We've seen how big brands buy up small independent operators (Coca Cola's purchase of Innocent smoothies, for example) so that they can gain traction with people who are mistrustful of large corporations, and how they use Instagram to set a whole host of consumer desires in motion.

For Mighty Advisors, intuition takes the place of big data and analytics (though many have a profound understanding of these tools as well). With their insights into how human beings work and their internal multidimensional maps of the complementary and conflicting concerns of different groups and the forces at work on them, Mighty Advisors have a grasp of the many and varied pressure points people will respond to. Mighty Advisors both ancient and modern have understood human psychology (though it may not always have been called that). Today, they also have access to all the tools of media experts and opinion formers. Advertising guru Rory Sutherland has recently explored people's unconscious motivations and how advertisers tap into these to persuade consumers to buy products. According to Sutherland, although we might think that logic or science should be able to explain the way that people behave, the truth is that irrationality governs what we do to a far greater degree than we imagine.[34] The Mighty Advisor has

---

34   R Sutherland, *Alchemy*

an almost magical ability to tap into this unpredictability.

Nudging

We also now know how much human behaviour and decision making can be skewed by organisational culture, which sometimes prevents organisations from working effectively. Richard Thaler and Cass Sunstein suggest that patterns of behaviour and decision making can be moved incrementally, ie nudged, toward better outcomes through careful consideration of the choice architecture, which includes, for example, the number of alternatives and the aids to decision making that are available. [35]

The Mighty Advisor is likely to have both an intuitive understanding of the choice architecture of an organisation and one based on experience, so they are well placed to identify where processes and structures need subtle adjustment. Ideally, this soft power will temper the degree of command and control an organisation needs to exert, supporting the leader in bringing about change in a way that does not feel threatening.

Each individual in an organisation will have their own agenda, their personal preferences and goals. The combination of these agendas in a larger grouping constitutes a macro environment within which members are continually exerting both conflicting and complementary pulls.

---

35   R Thaler and C Sunstein, *Nudge*

One of the Mighty Advisor's great political skills is exploiting this effect with key people. If you can get early agreement from them and a decision, you can control the juggernaut that is the complex modern organisation.

A GLANCING TOUCH

The uncertainty brought about by the Covid-19 pandemic made many companies realise that they could not simply carry on as before, but they had little idea of how they could adapt.

I have been brought in to, in effect, prophesise on the basis on the data, the capacity and ethos of the organisation that I have sensed through my wanderings and my experience-based intuition. I then suggest possibilities that strike a chord and the organisations pivot, finding renewed hope and impetus. They adopt new strategies to find more highly differentiated products and niche markets, making a commitment for the next seven to ten years – seeing the endgame rather than looking at the short-term horizon.

This means that Mighty Advisors often don't need to exert a great deal of pressure at all – a gentle nudge is all it takes. Picture a spinning top that can be sent off on a totally different trajectory with the lightest of touches – this

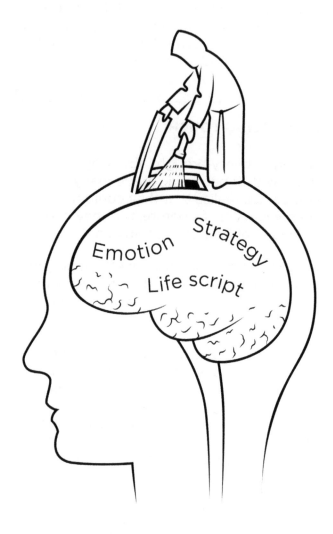

Mighty Advisors work inside the minds of leaders as close to the grey matter as possible

illustrates how a Mighty Advisor's intervention with a leader can be amplified. The dynamism of the leader, the momentum that makes them effective, can be harnessed with a figurative 'hand on the back' and amplified across a network, allowing the Mighty Advisor's influence to reverberate throughout an organisation.

Amplifying

In disseminating their influence across an organisation, the Mighty Advisor sparks a chain reaction radiating out from the leadership. The nudge they give the leader is transmitted onwards to key people in the organisation, people you could describe as 'nodes', defined by the Oxford English Dictionary as points 'in a network or diagram at which lines or pathways intersect or branch.'[36]

The Mighty Advisor's wanderings through an organisation or a community will have enabled them to identify people who, often unwittingly, act as nodes. These individuals may have a degree of responsibility and status in an organisation, but not necessarily; they could just be that congenial person from another team that we chat to because they seem to know what's going on everywhere and they always have a good story to tell. a strengthening in organisational values, a pivot in output, preparing staff for a merger – the groundwork for all such changes could

---

36 www.lexico.com/definition/node

be seeded though the network by such individuals, whom Malcolm Gladwell calls 'connectors' (see Chapter 4).

The Mighty Advisor may even come to 'mark' – in the footballing sense – certain people in an organisation, so that they can target their influence, either according to need or to type of message.

Manipulating

The word 'manipulate' has some rather negative connotations these days, but I prefer to think of it more in the context of holistic therapies and practices. As a teacher of yoga, I know that if you go up to someone in a yoga pose and adjust, say, the angle of an arm, with the lightest of touches you can bring their body into the correct alignment and enhance the benefits of their exercise. This type of manipulation is not Machiavellian or self-seeking; it is a skilled intervention to enhance the functioning of an individual, group, or organisation as a whole.

To continue the yoga analogy, it's as if the Mighty Advisor is running a yoga class with the leader out in front as the star practitioner whom the others will be trying to emulate. The Mighty Advisor will be advising the leader and correcting their posture, but at the same time looking out for others further back in the class to manipulate, because their location in the room or their relationship with others will facilitate the spread of good practice.

Influencing versus leading

The yoga instructor analogy leads us toward consideration of some alternative models of leadership that are relevant to the Mighty Advisor's role and also demonstrate the complementarity of the respective skills of the leader and Mighty Advisor.

Servant leader

In the yoga example, the Mighty Advisor is acting in the service of the group, watching for signs that help and guidance are needed, and responding accordingly. The term 'servant leader' was coined by Robert K Greenleaf,[37] inspired by Hermann Hesse's book *The Journey to the East*. The central character in this novel is Leo, a servant who accompanies a group of men on a mystical journey. He is ostensibly their servant, whose task it is to perform all the chores; he also keeps their spirits up with songs and the sheer force of his presence. When he disappears, the group falls apart. One of them is finally admitted to the holy order that sponsored the journey; there, he discovers that Leo is in fact the head of this order.

Greenleaf came to believe that great leadership was derived not from status or skill, but rather from the will of the individual to serve. This model inverts traditional concepts of leadership: the servant leader is focused not on increasing

---

37   RK Greenleaf, *Servant Leadership*

and consolidating their own power, but on inspiring and empowering those who work for them. They display humility instead of wielding authority and look for ways to foster creativity and a sense of purpose.

Servant leadership has ten characteristics: listening, empathy, healing, awareness, persuasion, conceptualisation, foresight, stewardship, commitment to the personal growth of others, and building community. Some of these are immediately recognisable as traits typical of the Mighty Advisor. We have discussed most of these characteristics elsewhere, but I must emphasise the importance of awareness. Much of the Mighty Advisor's ability to influence is derived from the trust the leadership and the organisation place in them to know what is going on. The effective Mighty Advisor is continually scanning the environment, consciously and unconsciously monitoring subtle changes, trends and power shifts, all the while adding to their knowledge and the resources they place at the disposal of the leader.

It's as if the Mighty Advisor is sitting in a massive CCTV control room, watching dozens of flickering screens to monitor what's going on. Somehow they are able to distinguish between activity that is innocuous and activity that need to be addressed, and they will direct the leader's attention accordingly. In change management terms, this approach allows for subtle, incremental tweaks in significant areas across the organisation that will have a greater impact than a wholesale effort in one department.

THE CONTROL ROOM

When I ran an organisation of 3,000 people, I did so based on one chart, a dashboard that answered my basic questions: 'Should I be anxious? Should I be on alert? Or can I go and have a gin and tonic?'

I often challenge a CEO to come up with a dashboard summarising the state of their organisation, but they tend to produce something that is far too low-level to be of real use. What I'm after is something more like I had the IT department at one pharma company create for me: software that generated a Jaguar-style dashboard giving political and cultural readouts alongside the more standard financial and production metrics. As well as the international economic context, I could also get a forecast on something as specific as the availability of suitable recruits for clinical trials.

Half mastermind and half sounding board, the Mighty Advisor harbours no overwhelming personal ambition; this means that their advice can be trusted. The leader and the Mighty Advisor form the perfect double act, since the Mighty Advisor in no way detracts from the leader's status and authority but supplies all the insight and intelligence (in the sense of information) that the leader is not usually in a position to cultivate.

The Mighty Advisor has the correct optics on an organisation

There is an alchemy at work when the leader
and the Mighty Advisor acting as servant leader
come together. The servant leader enables the
leader's followers to look beyond their own
ambitions and contribute collectively to the
group or the organisation.

Synergy

What makes this double act so effective is the
synergy between leader and Mighty Advisor.
Synergy is the term for the interaction or co-
operation of two or more elements to produce a
combined effect that is greater than the sum of
their separate effects. You can see this process
everywhere in the natural world, from the division
of labour in bacterial colonies to the behaviour
of socially organised groups like wolf packs.
These interactions have a catalytic effect not just
on the elements themselves, but on the entire
organisational system within which they exist.

For an insight into how the synergy between
the leader and the Mighty Advisor works, we
can turn to the work of Meredith Belbin, the
British management consultant and author
of *Management Teams*.[38] Based on extensive
research with teams, Belbin proposed that, to
work effectively, a team had to comprise eight
(later nine) key roles, and that most people
have a preferred leadership style. In looking
at the types of people who embraced these
different roles, he noted that some worked
particularly well together. To explore two key

38   M Belbin, *Management Teams*

roles Belbin identified as complementary, I think it's useful to return to the biological term 'phenotype' here, as it refers to the observable appearance and behaviour of an individual,

The first phenotype is that of the chairman, not in the formal governance sense, but as the individual who leads in a complex, problem-solving environment. They carry the responsibility for maintaining the structure of the organisation and delegating work. It's worth noting that this role has since been designated 'co-ordinator'.

The second phenotype is that of the shaper, who excels at galvanising the team to ensure that it does not become complacent and that it considers all the possibilities. The combination of the structural authority of the chairman and the disruptive energy of the shaper creates the ideal leader/Mighty Advisor partnership.

Shapers thrive in organisations that need change. Complexity and political caution in an organisation can cause paralysis. In this situation, the shaper, in Belbin's words, 'can ginger up a slow-moving system or even change the way in which they function'.[39] The Mighty Advisor as change agent is needed more than ever in a world where the rapid advances of technology may represent a known threat, but where more medieval forces, such as a pandemic, may still reassert themselves.

---

39   M Belbin, *Management Teams*

Triangulation

Someone who has been successful because they have adhered closely to their life script may be resistant to change. The fates of others who have attempted change may also serve to inhibit their preparedness to do so themselves. You can understand their misgivings in the face of a possible loss of control. The Mighty Advisor understands that the prospect of change can be met with deep-rooted resistance, with fear and ambivalence and a whole host of limiting beliefs. Personal fears can be amplified in an organisational setting to become systemic emotional fields. Like magnetic fields and gravitational fields, these are invisible to the naked eye, but they tend to control the functioning of individuals in an organisation to a greater degree than the overt rules and practices that people consciously subscribe to.

Psychiatry professor Dr Murray Bowen has suggested that anxiety moves throughout an organisational system via a mechanism that he terms 'triangulation': if fear arises in one person, it is immediately transferred to another, then picked up from the emotional field by a third, hence triangulation.[40] At work there is an evolutionary desire for togetherness, which has always been a prerequisite for survival. This means that people do not function as separate entities; they are permeable, allowing emotions to flow to and from. The chronically anxious organisation develops a herd identity,

---

40   M Bowen, *Family Therapy in Clinical Practice*

to which everyone is expected to adapt. The herd organisation discourages dissent, places more importance on feelings than ideas, values peace over progress and comfort over innovation. The status quo wins.

The Mighty Advisor must be able to say 'I' when others are saying 'we', holding fast to their own differentiation. If they can maintain an authentic, unperturbed presence in the face of others' anxiety, the benefits for the leader and the organisation are clear. The Mighty Advisor's capacity for differentiation means that they will never be one of an organisation's emotional dominoes.

KEEPING UP THE DISRUPTION

The triangulation effect often places me at odds with others in a group dynamic, but I hold fast, because it's my job to make sure that we keep the unexpected, the surprising option, on the table. It's easy enough to return to the well-trodden path at any time. My message to them is: 'You wanted a thought disrupter, so that's what I'm doing, and I'm going to keep doing it.'

I've seen this triangulation in board meetings where the management team is struggling to keep up with their investors who may be 'ganging up' on them. In this situation, my job is to break up the tension. By not taking sides, but asking honest, provocative questions, I've

averted the long-term political animosity
that can result in a dysfunctional board.

Groups and individuals are always looking for
scapegoats and people they can blame through
a process of triangulation. The Mighty Advisor
can avoid this fate by being slightly remote and
exerting influence from their position in the
shadows. What's more, the Mighty Advisor must
keep the leader differentiated. Fuelled by the
clarity of the Mighty Advisor's big picture,
the leader can deploy their authority to get the
organisation to respond appropriately to
the challenges that face them. The one-to-
one relationship between these two figures is
of central importance. Something instinctive
happens when a leader is with someone they
trust, a confidant, especially if their relationship
has been allowed to grow over a long period.

The *consiglieri*

First emerging in the 1950s, the concept of
'responsibility charting' reflected an approach to
work tasks based on four main roles: responsible,
accountable, consulted and informed. It may
seem like a cut and dried, MBA-type approach
to understanding teams, but it does give us
a simple language for discussing a complex
subject and is useful in getting to grips with
the influence of the Mighty Advisor.

In his book, *Consiglieri: Leading From the
Shadows* (*'consiglieri'* being the mafia term for

trusted advisor), Saatchi and Saatchi deputy chairman Richard Hytner examines leadership through the prism of two of these roles: A, the leader, and their relationship with C, those whom they consult. According to Hytner, the people the leader consults may be chiefs of staff, chief finance or operating officers etc, reflecting the range of specialisms needed to make an organisation work. Hytner describes the C role thus:

> 'It is easy to want the top job; less easy to know whether being the ultimate decision-maker is right for you. Do you really wish to be an A, the main attraction and the ace of absolute accountability, or might you prefer to be a key C, on whom the A depends, the kind of person who leads, influences, counsels, guides, and helps the A deliver?'[41]

It's incumbent on the leader to display charisma, conviction and self-assurance, to grasp situations quickly and take action, whereas the consultee can – and probably should – remain more low-key and understated in their behaviour. Hytner's description constitutes an identikit picture of most of the Mighty Advisors we've encountered in this book.

---

41   R Hytner, *Consiglieri*

Together, the leader and the Mighty Advisor
are a formidable duo. Despite (and sometimes
because of) a low-key or offbeat presence,
Mighty Advisors are talented practitioners of
the art of not only keeping the show on the
road but scanning the map and constantly
adjusting the route to make sure it is the
best one. But how do they go about nudging
people's thinking and seeding ideas to make
this happen? What is it that makes their
messages so compelling? In the next chapter,
we'll look at the Mighty Advisor's specialised
approach to language and communications.

6 The Mighty Advisor's ability to detect patterns in the apparently random flow of events means they can shape them into a meaningful narrative.

CHAPTER 6

Resonance And Ritual

A Mighty Advisor may have all the experience and wisdom in the world and the keenest intuition, but they need certain tools to translate these into influence and ultimately action. They understand very well how they are perceived by others and how their messages are received, so language and performance are key tools at their disposal. For some, their style of communication is their hallmark; others tailor their mode of address to the context, the audience, or the content of the message, knowing exactly which buttons to push and when. They are also able to tap into unseen and unheard channels. Though these are hard to pin down, they are a key part of the Mighty Advisor's unique ability to work equally well behind the scenes, at the hub of unobservable but powerful communications. Let's have a closer look at how the Mighty Advisor orchestrates language and spectacle for maximum impact.

Language

In the late 1930s, sales guru Elmer Wheeler came up with his famous maxim, 'Don't sell the steak, sell the sizzle.'[42] If you think about it

---

42   J McNulty, 'The Sizzle'

for a second, this makes perfect sense. There's nothing intrinsically appealing about a lump of dead animal but conjure up the sounds and smells of a steak cooking with the prospect of biting into its tenderness, and the deal is sealed. We see evidence of this approach all around us. Take a camera shop: it doesn't showcase the equipment – let's face it, one SLR camera looks much like another – it showcases the vivid images you will be able to capture once you own the equipment.

It is precisely the Mighty Advisor's knack of making what they say vivid and appealing that makes them such good communicators. They know how to take the most mundane or even unwelcome information and give it compelling imagery and a narrative arc. How do they do this?

Metaphor

The essence of a metaphor is that it's a way of understanding one phenomenon in terms of another. We use metaphor in everyday life to a remarkable degree, without even being aware of it. Think of how many terms from the tech industry have entered our ordinary language to enliven what we want to express: we talk of people being 'hardwired' to behave in certain ways, as if they were circuit boards, to convey the extent of various formative influences on them. Some people express a desire for an 'upgrade', if they are no longer satisfied with their home, car, or even partner.

Metaphors work through a process called isomorphism whereby, if the representation of an experience is similar enough to that original experience, it will trigger the same responses. The example commonly given to illustrate this is that a row of lights flashing in sequence can give the illusion of motion because it replicates our experience of travelling in the dark. This is the mechanism that allows metaphor to produce an 'Aha!' moment when we 'see the light'. The emotional connection that can be achieved in this moment is one of the Mighty Advisor's most potent tools for influencing others.

For examples of conscious deployment of metaphor we can again turn to master exponent of the art, Jonathan Van-Tam. In Chapter 4 I quoted his vivid analogy comparing (or rather not) the Covid vaccine to a yoghurt, but it's worth examining another example from his briefings: the endurance of lockdown and hope for release described as a wait for a train on a bleak platform. 'It's wet, it's windy, it's horrible... And two miles down the tracks, two lights appear and it's the train and it's a long way off and we're at that point at the moment.'[43]

With this metaphor, Van-Tam was able to establish an emotional connection with the audience. We have all had the experience of waiting miserably on a cold platform and felt the tide of relief when we finally glimpse the train in the distance, which is why his words resonate. We both understand and feel understood.

---

43   K Rawlinson, 'Bugles, shootouts, trains?'

Polemic

As a technique, polemic is almost exactly the opposite of metaphor. Where metaphor seeks to establish an emotional connection by referring symbolically to shared experience, polemic seeks to provoke and create distance.

The term 'polemic' derives from the Greek *polemikos*, meaning warlike or hostile. Intended to excite a strong reaction, polemic is a classic tool of thought disruption. The most notorious example is perhaps Jonathan Swift's pamphlet *A Modest Proposal*, first published in 1729, which suggests that impoverished Irish families should unburden themselves of their infants by selling them to the rich for food.[44] Swift's intention was, of course, to satirise indifference to the poor and attack the policy the British government had adopted towards Ireland by shocking people into realising what a logical extension of their indifference could look like. In this way, polemic can function as an extreme 'devil's advocate' mechanism, making it not unlike the brainstorming exercise that invites participants to think about what they would do if they wanted to achieve the opposite result from the one they are seeking.

Another mechanism through which polemic can work is exaggeration. A Mighty Advisor is likely to propose a radical solution to a problem knowing full well that no one in their right mind would agree to implement such a

---

44   J Swift, *A Modest Proposal*

solution. However, they will have opened up thinking on the subject to such a degree that, when they come back with a suggestion that is far less ambitious, it may be accepted with some relief. If the Mighty Advisor had made this same proposal initially, it would have seemed far-fetched. Now, in contrast to the outlandish original proposal, it seems positively timid.

This is an extremely useful technique to use when an organisation is stagnating, or when opposing factions have reached a gridlock in their disputes. Though it made him few friends, it's a technique that Dominic Cummings made effective use of in revitalising the Conservative Party. There's nothing like it for exciting engaged and passionate thought and for moving an organisation forward in its ambition and willingness to take a calculated risk.

Storytelling

We are all far more responsive to patterns than we aware of. When the view in front of us doesn't supply our eyes with enough of this, our brains will often fill in the blanks. Patterns give us a framework, something we can get a grip on, a sense of security.

The Mighty Advisor's ability to detect patterns in the apparently random flow of events in everyday life or within an organisation means they can shape them into a meaningful narrative. They recognise the power of the narrative arc, which broadly moves from the status quo being disrupted by the introduction of jeopardy, to a middle section in which the protagonists combat this jeopardy, and a resolution, which is not necessarily the same as happy ending. This concept of a story is something that we all relate to from our earliest years.

The Mighty Advisor may use this narrative arc to reveal to the leader their possible 'life script' in the context of their organisation: a tale of destiny that sees the leader identify what is wrong in the corporate body and take on the challenge of addressing the problem, achieving a resolution in the form of a newly energised, more confident and innovative organisation.

Along the way, the Mighty Advisor will be retelling this story of corporate development to different groups of stakeholders, shaping it according to their different priorities and galvanising support and engagement by presenting people with a purpose.

Positivity

Growing interest in the workings of the mind in the mid-nineteenth century saw the development of various approaches to influencing thinking. Mesmerists and hypnotists focused on penetrating the mind at the subconscious level, inducing trance states to tap into what they saw as hidden forces. Freud both built on and rationalised these approaches with his study of how childhood events shaped the adult, and in his resulting therapeutic methods.

The initial aim of these movements was to promote health and wellbeing, but practitioners soon spotted the potential of positive thinking for fuelling achievement and success. The 1920s saw the publication of two highly influential positive thinking books: Napoleon Hill's *Think and Grow Rich*, and Dale Carnegie's *How to Win Friends and Influence People*. These were followed in 1952 by Norman Vincent Peale's *The Power of Positive Thinking*, which proposed many techniques that we would recognise today, such as visualisation and affirmations, but in the context of a strong Christian faith. Keeping a firm positive mindset became a prerequisite for leaders to achieve success, and the successful Mighty Advisor was the one who could help them to maintain this attitude.

The Mighty Advisor excels in deploying positive psychology and confidence building and can guide organisations in using these approaches to nurture the talents of their people. Moving from the study of shamanic psychology to examining the psychology of Wall Street traders, American psychiatrist Ari Kiev described in *Trading to Win* his approach to helping high achievers in business enhance and maintain their performance. One particular focus of his work is on building visual imagery.

There are clear links here with neurolinguistics programming and the concept of priming, whereby people's thinking is directed by 'seeding' certain ideas using positive language. Words are the track that the mind train follows, so it's important to use the right ones. Well-chosen words can mean the difference between rejection, indifference and engagement.

The theatre of the Mighty Advisor

Performance is a perfect tool both for communicating content in a powerful and memorable way and for forming a bond between the people who witness that performance. This is why ceremonies and rituals can be important weapons in the Mighty Advisor's armoury. You can see performance deployed in this way at churches across the world: the church service is a ceremony designed to bond participants and reaffirm their spiritual commitment through (except for the most austere of sects) an appeal to the senses through music, participatory singing, archaic language, and sometimes scents.

The priest can be directly linked with the shaman and reflects a pattern that recurs across continents and cultures. The shaman is a figure close to the tribal leader, but with no leadership responsibility themselves. With wisdom forged through a journey of self-discovery, the shaman sees the world through a different lens, and can share that vision with the group to strengthen its sense of identity and commitment. In some cases, you can interpret the term 'vision' literally: in the *ayahuasca* ceremony in South America, hallucinogenics form part of the ritual.

This may not be a tool that the modern Mighty Advisor has recourse to, but the ritual gatherings of the corporate organisation can also benefit from the visionary input of someone outside the hierarchy and the creation of an ambience in which participants will be receptive.

*Copper carving of a Sámi shaman from
Norway with his drum*

THE MOTOR SHOW

I once led a large organisation that was very process-driven, as clinical organisations tend to be. Desperate to give its cautious, conservative culture a bit of a jolt, I arranged a bit of a surprise for them at our annual conference.

It was being held at a hotel outside Milan that was often used for fashion shows, so there were huge doors at the back of the room to allow for elaborate sets to be brought in. Once all the medics and clinical scientists – about 300 of them – were seated, the room was darkened, the doors opened and I drove in with an ear-splitting roar, at the wheel of a Dino Ferrari. Everybody went wild.

I certainly had their attention after that. What's more, I had opened up a sense of possibility: there was no need to stick with the same old same old – we could do things in a new, different way.

If you look back at the archetypes that I introduced at the beginning of the book, you'll notice quite a few figures with a theatrical flair: Helena Blavatsky, with her thrilling esoteric séances, for example, and Svengali with his impresario-style influence over Trilby. Another character from fiction who springs to mind is

Albus Dumbledore, chief wizard in the Harry Potter series, with his flamboyant outfits, his whimsical knitting and his penchant for staging set pieces to dazzle the Hogwarts pupils.

The average organisation regularly runs performative events. Some of them have a stated purpose that all participants understand and accept, such as the annual shareholders' meeting or a quarterly planning meeting, others are purely social, such as the office Christmas party, but they all have a function that goes beyond face value. These are perfect opportunities for the Mighty Advisor to ply their trade, and you could argue that a leader has an obligation to ensure that these organisational set pieces are not boring events dreaded by the participants, but ones that guarantee interest and engagement by whatever means possible: *coup de théâtre*, collective activity, emotional impact – the Mighty Advisor will know which to deploy.

Beyond words

I picture Mighty Advisors as having sensitive antennae, capable of picking up subtle signals. They are able to receive and broadcast on multiple wavelengths, choosing the right channel for their audience, be that one other individual or a mass gathering – with no words spoken. If these antennae were visible, they would probably look rather alarming. They are what make the Mighty Advisor's wanderings so fruitful; they are continuously receiving intelligence, alive to the subtlest changes in mood and cultural shifts. As the information comes in, it is stored for easy retrieval at a later date. It's the computations that the Mighty Advisor makes based on all this gathered intelligence that enables them to make such accurate predictions.

Prophecy

When the Mighty Advisor combines everything they have stored in their minds with their skills in detecting patterns, they have the means of predicting what is likely to happen. They may not have access to John Dee's obsidian mirror to reveal the future, but they have some equally powerful magic at their fingertips – experience, embodied intuition, big data – with which they can make their forecasts.

Everyone will have their favourite prophets, but those mentioned most frequently in despatches in recent years include Steve Jobs and Senator Elizabeth Warren, the woman who predicted the 2008 financial crash.[45]

Trust containers

There is a mysterious song by Bob Dylan called 'The Mighty Quinn'. Quinn, an Inuit, is a long-awaited figure who will make everyone jump for joy when he arrives. The lyrics never disclose what he does or why his presence is so transformative, but it's clear everyone feels better when he's there.

---

45 M Valverde, 'Elizabeth Warren says she warned about the financial crisis before it happened. That's true'

This is what I mean when I speak of the Mighty Advisor 'holding' the space of the group. Within an ordinary room, a Mighty Advisor can create a ritualistic space in which people will feel safe and confident. Even if the Mighty Advisor is not leading the main event, their presence alone generates an atmosphere of trust – an intangible benefit that is worth just as much as the specific experience or learning that they contribute.

As a communicator, the Mighty Advisor is second to none. Somehow managing to receive and transmit simultaneously, they pick up and make sense of the subtlest of signals, shaping them into compelling messages that engage the hearts and minds of leaders and inspire commitment and enthusiasm throughout organisations.

In the next chapter, we'll look at the complex networks through which the Mighty Advisor diffuses their influence, whether covert or overt.

The Mighty Advisor
is a master navigator
of the living typology
that embraces all
the individuals in an
organisation.

CHAPTER 7

Systemic Sensitivity

The Mighty Advisor's initial channel of communication may be with the leader, but their impact radiates outwards across an organisation and beyond, through both time and space. There is concrete evidence for this, no matter what your view of the consequences, in the legacy of John Dee, who in 1577 wrote a book setting out his vision of a maritime empire and arguing for Britain's right to claim territory in the New World. But my inspiration in thinking about how the Mighty Advisor can navigate the systems of the modern organisation is always Father Joseph, since it would be hard to find a web of intrigue more complex than the court of Louis XIII of France. I picture him wandering the corridors of Versailles developing his networks, building alliances and deploying his polymathic skills to steer the monarch (via Richelieu) through the minefield of political manoeuvring, espionage and religious tensions of the time.

The modern Mighty Advisor must have the same mental agility to be able juggle the daily realities of an organisation with the competing claims and changing priorities of the people within it.

Systems thinking

The increasing specialism of science has resulted in the tendency to break problems down into ever smaller parcels and adopt a reductionist, logical approach to solving them. We've ended up with a million jigsaw pieces and an intimate knowledge of the shape, boundary and image of each one, but little concept of the bigger picture that they add up to. In practical terms, this translates into, for example, elderly patients having to attend a variety of outpatient appointments for different ailments and being prescribed drugs that may work against one another and result in more sickness, when what is needed is for someone to take a holistic view of what is causing their illness.

Yet as far back as the 1950s, psychotherapist Fritz Perls proposed that we should look at patterns and configurations rather than at individual components, coining the term 'Gestalt'.[46] Gestalt therapy addresses the whole person, rather than individual symptoms.

As a systems thinker, the Mighty Advisor can see each component pixel clearly and how it relates to the whole: the big picture and the interconnectedness within that picture. This allows the Mighty Advisor to see a myriad of possibilities, taking into account all the factors and their possible ramifications simultaneously. It's the exact opposite of breaking the elephant down into manageable chunks, to use an

---

46   FS Perls, *Ego, Hunger and Aggression*

analogy that is frequently bandied about in a corporate context. The benefit of this holistic approach is that the decisions it leads to are far more robust, given that they are taken with the likely consequences in mind.

Dealing with complexity

With their ability to see the connections between apparently unconnected elements and the flow of influence and activity between them, it's as if the Mighty Advisor is always looking at a sophisticated network diagram. Most people will be familiar with these in some form, from a simple family tree to complex models of chemical structures. Network diagrams are a static representation of a dynamic reality. An organisation chart shows the division and direction of authority in an organisation. In a criminal network diagram, we can see the movement of illicit goods and money, and how blood ties are related to this. At a micro level, the interactome diagram shows the whole set of physical interactions between the molecules in a particular cell.

The Mighty Advisor has the rare ability to hold network diagrams at whatever scale in their mind and use them for navigation. They use network diagrams such as topographical maps to guide them in negotiating the terrain of a system or an organisation, but they are three-dimensional in that the Mighty Advisor will also be considering history and precedent alongside geography and using all these elements to forecast the probability of possible consequences.

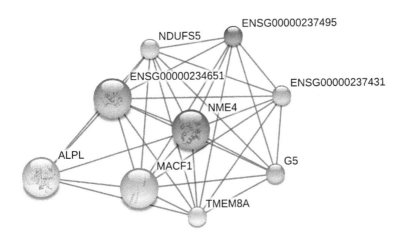

*Part of a protein interactome depicting the predicted
protein interactions of TMEM8A in humans*

There is no substitute for this perspective, as the unfortunate beginning of the Independent Inquiry into Child Sexual Abuse demonstrates: the first two heads appointed to the inquiry were both obliged to withdraw – Baroness Butler Schloss because her brother had been Attorney General at the time some of the abuses occurred, and Dame Fiona Woolf because of her friendship with one of the individuals under investigation. Where was the government advisor with a detailed understanding of the web of connections between the people at the top of their professions? An individual with the political nous to recognise how damaging it could be if there were any public perception of bias or the operation of an 'old boy' network likely to close ranks?

Systemic constellations

It was Austrian psychotherapist Bert Hellinger who first applied the idea of systems thinking to interpersonal relationships, creating a model he called 'systemic constellations' specifically for the purpose of examining family interactions.[47] His approach seems to have stemmed from the time he spent working in South Africa with Zulus, whose methodology for dealing with problems in the family was to take the individual's initial complaint and build a composite picture around it based on contributions from a number of other family members.

---

47   See https://systemicconstellations.com and
     www.hellinger.com/en/family-constellation

This modelling has been expanded further to include organisational systems and the relationships between the individuals within them. Systemic constellations in this context become a powerful mapping technique for bringing to the surface hidden dynamics in organisational relations. The resulting distinctive three-dimensional shape of these dynamics is what Albrecht Mahr, psychoanalyst and specialist in political constellations and peace and reconciliation work, calls the 'Field'.[48]

The Mighty Advisor is a master navigator of the Field. They understand this living typology that embraces all the individuals in an organisation and the relative strength and weakness of their relationships, and can predict how the Field will change as a result of people leaving or joining the group.

Systemic awareness is being able to feel and resonate with what is happening in a group. The group is always greater than the sum of its parts and, as it grows, its internal configuration changes, as people cluster round different individuals. We can see this process at work most clearly in political parties as factions form, splinter and re-form, with repercussions for wider alliances and decision making.

Understanding organisations

In getting to grips with an organisation I often imagine myself removing the outer wall of its

---

48   A Mahr, 'How the living and the dead can heal each other'

building and being able to observe all at once the movements of the individuals inside – who is having a tête-a-tête with whom, who is in the animated group clustered round the tea point. (The most recent challenge, of course, is to plot how to replicate this in the world of Zoom and Microsoft Teams.)

In any organisation, people want to preserve their individuality and their agency, but they need to function as an integrated part of an existing or evolving whole. This tension is part of the dynamic, as is the fact that, no matter how quickly an organisation develops, it will always bear the imprint of former leaders.

A DAY IN THE LIFE

Although every client is different, my way of working with the leaders, engaging with individuals across a hierarchies and departments and sensing the undercurrents swirling around the organisation follows a tried and tested pattern (that I occasionally turn on its head, of course).

I regularly spend a whole day with each organisation. My first meeting will be with the CEO, for an update on what's happening. I want them to talk – to tell me everything that's on their mind. Through subtle questioning, I nudge them towards the bigger picture: the consequences of their concerns and how these concerns join up to create the climate of the organisation. What I'm aiming for is evidence from them that adds up to something like the Minard map featured in Chapter 4, though they often have difficulty articulating such a comprehensive picture and revert to itemising tactical worries.

Having done the groundwork with the leader, I'll head off to the coffee machine with my antenna absorbing the ambient atmosphere. Once I know who goes where and when, I might even plan this excursion quite precisely, so that I can be sure of running into individuals whose perspective on the organisation I might find useful.

Following this, I'll have a series of one-to-one meetings with my 'nodes', the well-connected people with influence. They may not necessarily be particularly senior, but they're people I've identified as 'spreaders': what they say and do ripples through the organisation, and people – often subconsciously – view them as role models. I know that what I'll get from them is a frank and perceptive picture of what's really going on.

My final port of call is usually a formal meeting; it could be a portfolio review body, or a commercial strategy group, or a board of some kind. I might be a member of whichever grouping it is, or I might be present only as an observer. Sometimes I'm there to ask the awkward questions – questions such as, 'Why are you still working on this project after ten years when nobody is interested in it?' in relation to something that may be close to the CEO's heart but has no commercial potential. Others might not feel able to challenge a pet project in this way, but that's what I'm there for.

Sometimes I'm there to mitigate, or contextualise, difficult messages from the senior team. Because of my rapport with various people on the boards or project groups, the resistance they might feel to messages handed down from on high dissipates if it has been filtered through me, as they have come to know and trust me. Partly, this is because I can speak both as a scientist and as someone with commercial acumen, enabling me to defuse the age-old tension between specialists and generalists.

On any given day I might also be involved in other activities: contributing to a pitch deck for investors, coaching an individual for a specific event, or 'holding' an organisation that is going through a difficult patch by being a responsive sounding board (or punching bag, if need be) for a senior team facing tough decisions and conversations.

So there you have it, a typical day in the life of this Mighty Advisor – though no two days are ever alike!

Leadership expert Peter Senge has proposed that organisations are living systems that behave like biological systems. His book *The Fifth Discipline* describes them as fluid systems that are in a state of continuous adaptation and improvement.[49] They have a fixed boundary, within which are many entities (the people) that exchange information. Just as in a natural ecosystem, removal of a specific component can cause a cascade of effects and immense disruption; the rate of flux can speed up or slow down, depending on the rigidity of the system. A degree of flexibility is needed to allow the organisation to flex with prevailing influences, as rigidity will cause the structure to collapse. By way of analogy, think of the degree of 'give' needed in tall buildings to stop them from fracturing under the pressure of high winds.

Hidden architecture

Every organisation has a formal structure that its people are familiar with, usually depicted as a family tree-type diagram, with the hierarchies and operational silos clearly marked. As a result, it's hardly surprising that groups of people within organisations display territorial behaviour. Directors of departments or functional line managers can be fiercely protective of their departments; they defend their budgets and guard their territory, but there will always be influences at work that they have no control over. Identifying the source of these influences is key to understanding the hidden architecture

49   P Senge, *The Fifth Discipline*

of an organisation. The number of major influencers in any given organisation is quite small, but the Mighty Advisor knows exactly who those people are. They form the primary building blocks of the organisation.

It's here that 'small world' theory comes into play. This theory is illustrated by the concept of six degrees of separation, which holds that any two people on earth are only six or fewer acquaintances apart from each other. If this applies globally, how much smaller is the world of an organisation?

The Mighty Advisor is able not only to identify the highly connected individuals in an organisation but, because they understand the network, they also know where the nodes or hubs are through which ideas and influences are disseminated in different directions. In communications terms, it is far better to seed information through these networks and gather the response than to rely on top-down communications from the leader and a formal (and therefore inhibited) feedback process.

One of the first things I do when I go into an organisation is to ask the CEO, 'Who should I meet?' Inevitably, they will list heads of department. But as I start talking to these people, there are individuals whose names come up repeatedly and I realise that these are the people I really need to speak to, because they will be able to help me join the dots. They often also act as useful corrective to the official line coming from the C-suite.

I know that when I'm walking through an organisation with a CEO, they can't always sense what is going on, seeming to have little contact with their people. Others, though, are interacting with people all the time; they're watching the organisation, absorbing the atmosphere and picking up on the invisible currents flowing through it. People within an organisation tend to arrange themselves into recurring patterns. There's always at least one awkward person who has been there for years, is extremely discontented but has never summoned up the courage to leave. I'm sure you've come across people like this. This one disgruntled individual can do a lot to block the momentum of an organisation, so it helps to know who they are and, just as importantly, who is in their network.

A CEO who is alive to the networks in their organisation could probably draw you a good criminal network style map of their organisation. All I have to do is give them a piece of paper with a circle on it, and a name in the circle, say 'Sarah'. Then I ask them where they would place a circle with the name 'Fred' in it. They know exactly where it should go, though it may be at this point that they realise it would be better if these two particular individuals were not so close. Modern business books in general, and organisational development in particular, seem to me to focus on a far too superficial level. Change can only take place, and be sustained, if you can break up and disperse malign influences (such as Fred and Sarah seem to be) and foster and reinforce links between those whose positive narratives and energy can propel an organisation forward.

When I'm trying to change an organisation, I look for six or seven influencers who, if they are aligned with the direction of the organisation, can take others with them in that direction. They represent more than their talent, their specialism or their diligence: they have the capacity to make people fall in behind them. Sometimes they may not even be aware that they have this effect, but they are no less powerful for it.

TALENT SPOTTING

I undertook a big change project with a pharma company in France that employed hundreds of people. It had been trying to drive change for some time without success and decided finally to ask for some outside help.

The first thing I did was to engineer a situation that would allow me to identify the spreaders and influencers. At a conference of the company in question, I was able to observe different people presenting ideas. The fact that it was all in French proved to be a help rather than a hindrance, because I was able to focus on the persona of each individual and how they resonated with their audience rather than the content of their presentation. I then chose a handful of people as core influencers to work with, creating a group I called the 'Agents de Change'. The group received regular briefings from the senior leadership, but it was up to them how they spread the information they received through the organisation. One of the things they decided on was a poster exhibition, and because it was 'home grown' it had a freshness that was far more compelling than any slick internal communications campaign.

In my experience, within any group of a hundred people, there will be three to five influencers. Previously, I explained how revealing people's choice of where to position themselves in a room is. There is a practical exercise I run in a lot of the organisations that I work with, because it always yields useful results. I get twenty people in a room and ask them to walk around until they find a place where they feel comfortable and stop there. Some people are happy to be in a fairly isolated position at the edge of the room. Others want to be closer to their colleagues, in the middle of the room and perhaps even situated on the natural trajectory between one entrance and another. I can see from this that they are already well connected and that they are physically putting themselves in a position where they will be able to grow these connections. Although I make sure I get permission from the leader to talk to everyone in an organisation, I focus my efforts on these individuals, building a strong rapport with them. There comes a point, of course, when I need to move on. By this time, I will have reconfigured the leader's relationship with these influencers, so that there is a strong bond between them. Although it can be hard for an HR department to see that there is a justification for a promotion, or the creation of a new post to exploit their talents, the leader needs to ensure that the influencer's contribution is rewarded.

Some people, though, would find a promotion most unwelcome: their engagement with and enjoyment of the organisation derive from their current role, and it would be wise not to disrupt this dynamic. In such cases, the leader simply needs to allow them to flourish and to signal their value to the organisation as an individual. It might present a bit of a challenge in terms of a job title, since both organisations and society at large like to pigeonhole people, but it's important to endorse their right to roam and to make eclectic contributions to the organisation.

Strategy

It is now accepted that the first thing a CEO has to do when taking over a new organisation is make a lot of changes. They would be seen as being somehow remiss in their duties if they didn't embark on a restructure. But this 'ground zero' approach can be counterproductive, and this is where a Mighty Advisor can shape strategy in such a way as to retain what is of value while also galvanising transformation.

Leaders have usually attained their exalted position by having a vision for their organisation or within their industry, so it's frustrating for them when their teams fail to grasp the big picture. 'Why don't they get it? They just want to stay in their silos and protect their own turf,' is a common complaint. Departmental stubbornness spells disaster for organisational strategy. The etymology of 'strategy' has military origins, referring to the art of conducting warfare while factoring in a degree of uncertainty. The meaning developed over the centuries, coming in the nineteenth century to refer to political manoeuvring. In the twenty-first century, we have tended to apply it freely to anything and everything, from saving the planet to advancing to the next stage in a video game.

A serious strategy needs to set out a goal, or a series of goals, the actions needed to achieve them and how to marshal the resources to execute the necessary actions. The Mighty Advisor understands that thinking strategically should be a social experience – the act of sharing insights with colleagues brings a deeper dimension to the process and helps dispel the illusion that we are all separate entities acting independently.

In any effective strategy, all the elements will be connected in a logical sequence of cause and effect, though with enough flexibility to accommodate a range of possible outcomes. It's easy to assume that strategic thinking is an analytical left-brain process – that if you put in enough diverse data you will come up with the right answer. But this on its own is not enough. You still need to have a grasp of the whole picture, an ability to co-exist with the inescapable paradoxes and ambiguity of real life and a willingness to follow a hunch.

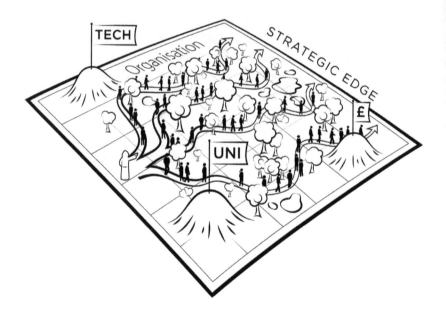

*Wandering and navigating the whole system gives
the Mighty Advisor a unique perspective*

Any strategy will have to reflect the aspirations and ambitions of the individuals in the organisation, as well its official mission, product or purpose. A commercial organisation will certainly contain many people for whom 'winning' is their chief aspiration. Historian and philosopher James Carse proposed that there are two kinds of games that people play: finite and infinite.[50] Players of the finite game are intent on winning; those playing the infinite game just want the game to continue. In large organisations, finite games are played within an infinite game. Examples of a finite game might be a successful project or an achievable strategy. There may not always be a great financial benefit to the organisation, but every win will count in reputational terms. Finite players abide by strict rules; unless they do so, they can't say who has lost or won. The aim of the infinite game is to keep the organisation and all the individuals in it in play. Infinite players constantly adjust the rules of the game in response to changing circumstances. German author Hermann Hesse understood the deep-rooted and compelling nature of the game. In *The Glass Bead Game* he envisages a game based on the synthesis of all arts and sciences; players progress through it by detecting hidden connections between unrelated elements.

The Mighty Advisor is skilled at both types of game and understands the interaction and ideal balance between the two. That balance will vary according to the type of organisation.

---

50   JP Carse, *Finite and Infinite Games*

A tech company, for example, advances by playing a series of finite games: releasing a new product, innovating, then superseding the new product. By contrast, a public service entity, such as a local council or a university, needs to excel at the infinite game, continually demonstrating their necessity.

The success of an organisation, be it an ebullient commercial company, a revered academic institution or anything in between, is the apotheosis of the Mighty Advisor's skill. They have the ability to cut through protocol and custom to relate to all the individuals in an organisation at a direct, personal level. They combine this with the capacity to apprehend the entire constellation of that organisation to enable them to develop a unique insight into the organisation and exert leverage through harnessing the hidden but powerful influences at work in any group of human beings.

Conclusion

We've covered a lot of ground since the exploration of the Mighty Advisor archetypes at the beginning of the book and I hope by now you're convinced of the value of a Mighty Advisor in some capacity. Perhaps some possible candidates have come to mind, even from within your own organisation.

It's easy to spot the difference between an organisation that benefits from a Mighty Advisor and one that doesn't. Management consultants may give you an efficient structure and a sound financial plan, but they can't get behind the veil of an organisation to pick up on the unspoken currents and influences that give any group of people its distinct identity. Without being able to get the measure of the group, it's impossible to engage all the individuals within it and take them with you.

There is an openness to the organisation with leadership enlightened enough to welcome the perceptiveness and sensitivity of the Mighty Advisor. Its members will feel their connectedness to the influences large and small that run through the organisation and that swirl around it in the outside world, and its responsiveness to them. Instead of the boundaries of a stultifying organisation, they will see the far horizons of infinite possibility. They will also feel the recognition of the collective and of the individual within the collective. Nothing fosters disengagement and apathy faster than the sense that what you have to offer is being spurned. The organisation that overtly encourages disruption, dissent and discussion will be able to tap into levels of imagination and innovation in its members that would otherwise be overlooked.

The problem is that leaders often find that they can't define the Mighty Advisor they're looking for – but they will recognise one when they turn up. The form this individual will take is wholly unpredictable and, when they first appear, people often don't know what to make of them. I know this because I've had endless debates with people who clearly don't know what to make of me: 'What are you, Tony? Are you a guru? Are you a sage?' (I've even had 'Are you a druid?') Yet other organisations I work with don't seem to see me as such a mystical figure; instead, I get called 'Uncle Tony'. But my favourite title of all has to be 'Cartographer of the Lesser-known Regions' – that really does make me feel like some kind of shaman!

People are beginning to realise there is more to a company than the bottom line. How else to explain, for example, the popularity of TED Talks? Why are self-help books so popular? Why is Waterstones full of books with titles like *Think Like a Monk*?

Further evidence that people now want more from organisations than a purely rational, transactional approach can be found in

Frédéric Laloux's *Reinventing Organizations*,[51] which charts the move from a cold, hierarchical body to one that is community-spirited and self-regulating – the Teal organisation – which you could describe as the ultimate goal of the Mighty Advisor.

We've already acknowledged that the modern organisation must give due weight to soft power, to the feminine principle. Alongside that, I'd like to see far more recognition of women as Mighty Advisors. Let's elevate women like Theodora (500–548 CE), wife of and a chief advisor to the Eastern Roman emperor Justinian, to the canon of sages and *éminences grises*. And what about Christine de Pizan (1364–1430), known as a prolific writer whose influence has continued to resonate, but also a figure close to the French court and purveyor of wisdom to the Dauphin? This historical recognition would pave the way for wider acknowledgement of their ongoing contribution to government, business, science and culture. Indeed, one might consider Kamala Harris, though undoubtedly an effective leader in her own right, as a Mighty Advisor to President Joe Biden; she certainly brings unique intergenerational and interracial insights to the White House.

If we needed any further convincing that organisations are ripe for disruption, consider Covid-19 and the extent to which the pandemic upended working and commercial practices

---

51   F Laloux, *Reinventing Organizations*

around the globe. The belief that you could not let your employees work from home for any length of time was swept away overnight. People had to be given a huge amount of autonomy and they rewarded the trust placed in them by demonstrating how constructively self-regulating they could be.

The pandemic also introduced new ways of apprehending an organisation. It might not have been possible to wander around, eavesdrop, note alliances, observe behaviour and generally pick up the vibe in a building, but Zoom and Microsoft Teams etc offered different opportunities for acquiring insights. My fantasy of a CCTV-type control room offering the Mighty Advisor an overview (not unlike the Marauder's Map used by some of the pupils at Hogwarts) through a myriad of screens almost became a reality. What the Mighty Advisor gains in this context is an insight into the non-professional facets of those in a meeting – including their aesthetic choices and the reading that occupies their minds. An almost entirely new field of divination has opened up for Mighty Advisors.

The time is right for organisations to embrace a way of working that is attuned to their unique ethos and offers their people opportunities for individuation, for coming into their own in terms of creativity and strength. In return, they contribute so much more than might have been thought possible.

I hope you have been intrigued, enlightened, stimulated, perhaps even annoyed by this exploration of the Mighty Advisor and what they have to offer the modern organisation. I'd love to get your feedback. If you feel like joining the discussion, head to www.thoughtdisruptor.com and leave a comment. I'm always up for having my own thoughts disrupted.

If you're interested in taking it a stage further and seeing how this approach could revolutionise your organisation, get in touch with me and together we can peer behind the veil, see what's really going on and tap into the currents that will sweep you into the future.

We've come to the end of the book, but there is never an end to the Mighty Advisor's work. There is always more to learn, process and feed back into my practice. This is perhaps why I'm so attached to the image of the *ouroboros*, an ancient Egyptian symbol representing the cycle of life, death and rebirth, which I'll leave you with now.

References

Belbin, M, *Management Teams: Why they succeed or fail* (Routledge, 2010)

Blavatsky, HP, *Isis Unveiled* (Quest Books, 1994)

Bowen, M, *Family Therapy in Clinical Practice* (Jason Aronson, 1993)

Campbell, J, *The Hero with a Thousand Faces* (New World Library, 2012)

Carnegie, D, *How to Win Friends and Influence People* (Vermilion, 2006)

Carse, JP, *Finite and Infinite Games* (Free Press, 2013)

De Bono, E, *Po: Beyond yes and no* (Penguin, London 1973)

De Bono, E, *Six Thinking Hats* (Penguin, 2016)

De Quincey, C, *Deep Spirit: Cracking the Noetic code* (The Wisdom Academy Press, 2008)

Du Maurier, G, *Trilby* (Oxford University Press, 2005)

Fischer, M, Bolz, P, and Kamel, S, *Adolf Bastian and his Universal Archive of Humanity: The origins of German anthropology* (Olms Verlag, 2007)

Fort, A, *Prof: The life of Frederick Lindemann* (Jonathan Cape, 2003)

Gladwell, M, *Blink: The power of thinking without thinking* (Penguin, 2006)

Gladwell, M, *The Tipping Point: How little things can make a big difference* (Abacus, 2002)

Greenleaf, RK, *Servant Leadership: A journey into the nature of legitimate power and greatness* (Paulist Press, 2002)

Heinlein, RA, *Stranger in a Strange Land* (Hodder, 2007)

Hesse, H, *The Glass Bead Game* (Vintage Classics, 2000)

Hill, N, *Think and Grow Rich* (Vermilion, 2004)

Huxley, A, *Grey Eminence* (Vintage Classics, 2005)

Hytner, R, *Consiglieri: Leading from the shadows* (Profile Books, 2019)

Jung, C, *The Archetypes and the Collective Unconscious* (Routledge, London 1991)

Kantor, J, 'An old hometown mentor, still at Obama's side', *New York Times* (23 November 2008), www.nytimes.com/2008/11/24/us/politics/24jarrett.html

Kiev, A, *Trading to Win: The psychology of mastering the markets* (John Wiley & Sons, 1998)

Lachman, G, *Madame Blavatsky: The mother of modern spirituality* (Penguin, 2012)

Laloux, F, *Reinventing Organizations: A guide to creating organizations inspired by the next stage of human consciousness* (Nelson Parker, 2014)

Mahr, A, 'How the living and the dead can heal each other', *The Knowing Field*, 6 (June 2005)

Marx, A, *My Life with Groucho: A son's eye view* (Robson Books, 1992)

McNulty, J, 'The sizzle', *The New Yorker* (16 April 1938), www.newyorker.com/magazine/1938/04/16/the-sizzle

Morton, B, 'Jonathan Van-Tam's best analogies: Penalties, equalisers and yoghurts', *BBC News* (3 December 2020), www.bbc.co.uk/news/uk-55169801

Parkinson, HJ, 'Canvas of lies: What Dominic Cummings' dress sense tells us about Brexit', *The Guardian* (13 September 2019), www.theguardian.com/fashion/2019/sep/13/canvas-of-lies-what-dominic-cummings-dress-sense-tells-us-about-brexit

Peale, NV, *The Power of Positive Thinking* (Vermilion, 1990)

Perls, FS, *Ego, Hunger and Aggression: The beginning of Gestalt therapy* (Random House, 1969)

Portes, R, 'Who needs experts?', *Think at London Business School* (9 May 2017), www.london.edu/think/who-needs-experts

Rawlinson, K, 'Bugles, shootouts, trains? Covid vaccine hopes prompt strained analogies', *The Guardian* (9 November 2020), www.theguardian.com/politics/2020/nov/09/bugles-shootouts-trains-covid-vaccine-hopes-prompt-strained-analogies

Reality Check Team, 'Dominic Cummings: Fact-checking the row' (BBC News, 2020), www.bbc.co.uk/news/52828076

Scharmer, CO, *The Essentials of Theory U: Core principles and applications* (Berrett-Koehler Publishers, 2018)

Senge, PM, *The Fifth Discipline: The art and practice of the learning organisation* (Random House, 2006)

Smith, D, *Rasputin: Faith, power and the twilight of the romanovs* (Picador, 2017)

Sorensen, R, *Thought Experiments* (Oxford University Press, 1999)

Sutherland, R, *Alchemy: The surprising power of ideas that don't make sense* (WH Allen, 2019)

Swift, J, *A Modest Proposal* (Penguin Classics, 2009)

Taylor, G, Jowett, J, Bourus, T, and Egan, G, *The New Oxford Shakespeare: Modern critical edition* (Oxford University Press, 2016)

Tesla, N, *My Inventions: The autobiography of Nikola Tesla* (Merchant Books, 2019)

Tesla, N, 'Some personal recollections', *Scientific American*, 112/23 (1915), 537, 576–577, www.jstor.org/stable/26022227?seq=1

Thaler, R, and Sunstein, C, *Nudge: Improving decisions about health, wealth and happiness* (Penguin, 2009)

Walker, A, 'John Major takes aim at Dominic Cummings for "poisoning" politics', *The Guardian* (5 September 2019), www.theguardian.com/politics/2019/sep/05/john-major-takes-aim-at-dominic-cummings-for-poisoning-politics

Whately, F (director), *David Bowie: The last five years* (BBC, 2017)

Vahimagi, T, 'Street-Porter, Janet (1946-)', *BFI Screenonline* (no date), www.screenonline.org.uk/people/id/1052094/index.html

Valverde, M, 'Elizabeth Warren says she warned about the financial crisis before it happened. That's true', *PolitiFact* (30 April 2019), www.politifact.com/factchecks/2019/apr/30/elizabeth-warren/elizabeth-warren-says-she-warned-about-financial-c

Further Reading

For anyone interested in following up on the fictional Mighty Advisors featured in the book and others, these titles will give you the full story.

Conan Doyle, A, *The Complete Sherlock Holmes Collection* (Wordsworth Editions, 2017)

Hesse, H, *Journey to the East* (Pilgrims Publishing, 2002)

Horton, C, Hidalgo, P and Zehr, D, *The Star Wars Book* (Dorling Kindersley, 2020)

Malory, T, *Le Morte d'Arthur, Volumes One and Two* (Penguin, 2004)

Martin, GRR, *A Song of Ice and Fire*, seven volumes (HarperCollins, 2012)

Rowling, JK, *Harry Potter: The complete collection* (Bloomsbury, 2018)

Tolkien, JRR, *The Hobbit* (HarperCollins, 2013)

Tolkien, JRR, *The Lord of the Rings Trilogy* (HarperCollins, 1995)

Acknowledgements

Thank you to all my loving family, not forgetting my two amazing aunts, Auntie Bill and Auntie Gwen, whose imagination, encouragement and sheer sense of fun have continued to inspire me throughout my life.

Thank you to so many individuals who have been my Mighty Advisors and sent me off on a different trajectory through their wise words and actions.

The Author

 Tony Sedgwick is a polymath, scientist, leader, serial entrepreneur, businessman, martial artist, yoga teacher, shamanic and systemic constellation practitioner, thought disruptor, and mighty advisor. He has spent his career in the life science sector working with high-functioning individuals who run complex organisations and businesses. He works on strategy, which he is sure lies in the grey matter of the brains of senior leaders. His specialism is understanding the 'big game' and how to play it.

Contact

🌐 www.thoughtdisruptor.com

in www.linkedin.com/in/tony-sedgwick-335b8a

🐦 @thoughtdisrupt